democracy
a beginner's guide

david beetham

ONEWORLD

OXFORD

democracy: a beginner's guide

Oneworld Publications
(Sales and editorial)
185 Banbury Road
Oxford OX2 7AR
England
www.oneworld-publications.com

© David Beetham
First South Asian Edition 2006

*This edition is for sale in the
Indian subcontinent only.
Not for export elsewhere.*

ISBN 1–85168–363–1

Cover design by the Bridgewater Book Company
Typeset by Jayvee, Trivandrum, India
Printed and bound in India by Gopsons Papers Ltd., Noida

Also author of:
Democratic Audit of the U.K. (now @ LSE)
Legitimation of Power (1991)
Representation
⊕ Self Citizen Participation NW

democracy

a beginner's guide

contents

tables and figures

tables

figures

preface and acknowledgements

What is democracy? What are its key features? Why are so many people in the 'old' democracies of the West disillusioned with it? Why is it so difficult to consolidate democratic government in other parts of the world? How can international organisations be democratised, if at all? What can we do to improve the quality of our own democracies?

These are the kinds of question this book will discuss. Chapters 1 and 2 discuss the definition and justification of democracy, and explore what is needed to realise it in practice at the level of the national state. These two chapters are relatively positive and 'upbeat' in tone. In more critical vein, chapters 3 and 4 explore the sources of disillusion with democracy in the 'old' democracies, and the problems of achieving sustainable democratic government in the rest of the world. Chapter 5 assesses schemes for extending democracy to the international sphere. Chapters 6 and 7 review attempts to re-engage citizens with government through innovations in participatory democracy, and ask what we can do as citizens to contribute to democratic renewal. I have then added a substantial glossary of key terms used in democratic discourse, which can form a guide to democracy in its own right. This is followed by a list of useful organisations and web-sites for readers to access if they wish.

The book is the fruit of more than two decades of teaching about democracy to students, practitioners and activists. Much of what I have learnt has come from their questions and insights, especially from those living in the 'new' democracies. I have more specific debts to acknowledge to a number of people who have commented on draft chapters, especially to John Schwarzmantel and Stuart Weir; and to Jules Townshend, who commented on the text as a whole. Any remaining defects are of course my own responsibility. I owe a particular debt to Iain Kearton, who prepared the tables and figures. Finally, I wish to thank Victoria Roddam, of Oneworld Publications, who invited me to write the book, and who has been both a support and an effective gadfly ever since.

David Beetham, September 2004

introduction: what is democracy?

What is democracy? You probably already have your own answer to this question. Most people do. The trouble is, their answers tend to be quite different from one another. Here, for example, is a list of some of the things people have called 'democracy' over the past fifty years or so: rule of the people, rule of the people's representatives, rule of the people's party, the well-being of the people, majority rule, dictatorship of the proletariat, maximum political participation, élite competition for the people's vote, multi-partyism, political and social pluralism, equal citizenship rights, civil and political liberties, a free or open society, a civil society, a free market economy, whatever we do in the UK or USA, the 'end of history', all things bright and beautiful.

What explains this enormous variety of meanings? One reason is that there are many different facets to democracy in practice, and people are isolating one element and treating it as if it were the whole. Another reason is that, because we are all in favour of democracy, it has become the most general term of approval in the political lexicon, and so has become emptied of all content; democracy is whatever we choose it to mean. Even the most ruthless dictators will claim the mantle of democracy, because they are carrying out the 'true will of the people'; dictatorship is just their country's own distinctive way of practising democracy!

No one is against democracy today, and everyone claims to be 'democratic'. It was not always so. In the eighteenth and nineteenth centuries there were many opponents of democracy, who believed it was a thoroughly bad thing. But at least they agreed with democracy's supporters what it actually was; they just disagreed about how to value it as a way of running society. These value disagreements still exist today, but they have become disguised as disagreements about what democracy *means*, since no one will come out openly and say that they are against it. So let us go back and try to recover an original meaning to the idea of democracy, and consider why its opponents thought it was such a bad thing. I shall start as simply as I can.

the meaning of democracy

Democracy can be most simply understood as a procedure for taking decisions in any group, association or society, whereby all members have an equal right to have a say and to make their opinions count. In life we take many decisions as individuals – where and how to live, what job to pursue, how much of our income to spend, what to spend it on, and so on. But as soon as we join with others in some common activity or enterprise, then decisions have to be taken for the group or association as a whole: who should be a member, what rules should be followed, what goals or policies should be pursued, how any necessary income should be raised or work distributed. We could call these 'collective decisions', in contrast to the individual decisions outlined above.

Now it is a standard feature of collective decisions to be taken at any level, from the smallest group or association up to society as a whole, that people disagree about them. So some procedure or decisional rule is required to determine how such disagreements should be resolved, and who is allowed to take part in doing so. In most associational life throughout human history the vast majority of those affected by collective decisions have been excluded from any participation in them. Decisions have been the preserve of a very few: the wisest, the oldest, the wealthiest, the most expert, or simply those with the most physical force at their disposal to coerce the rest. As forms of societal rule or government these examples of rule by the few have carried distinctive names such as aristocracy, meritocracy, oligarchy, and so on. And where decisions have been the preserve of a single individual, the system of rule has historically been called a monarchy.

In contrast to these historically recurrent forms of collective decision making by one or a few persons on behalf of the rest, democracy involves the principle that all members of an association or society should have the right to take part equally in the decisions that affect them. Democracy is based on the following key ideas:

- All members have interests that are affected by collective decisions.
- Everyone (by the time they are adult) is capable of reaching a view about what the best or least bad decision would be, both for themselves and for the association as a whole.
- The best decisions over the long run will be ones where all such views have been publicly aired and debated.
- Where debate and discussion fail to produce a single agreed outcome, decisions should be taken by a vote of all participating members.
- The principle of 'one person, one vote, one value' reflects a wider conception that all persons are of equal worth.

Naturally, these ideas require further discussion, and will be elaborated on during the course of the book. It is worth pointing out straightaway, however, that they have historically only very rarely been either believed in or practised. Even in ancient Athens of the fifth and fourth centuries BC, which gave us the word 'democracy' (rule by the common people, 'kratos' by the 'demos'), the 'people' did not include either women or slaves, both of whom were believed to be naturally inferior to male citizens. Indeed, it would have been impossible in practice for male citizens to have devoted the time they did to the collective affairs of their city, if there had not been a large supporting cast working full time on domestic and economically productive activities.

Despite this serious limitation, however, ancient Athens, and its democratic allies in cities across the Aegean, provided two key features which have been an inspiration to democrats ever since. The first was an effective working example of a popular assembly, in which ordinary citizens debated and decided laws and policies for their society in person, including issues of peace and war. Other democratic practices included the rotation of citizens in turn, selected by lot, to serve on an executive body or council, and to act as jurors in the courts. This model of popular self-government, of people controlling their own common affairs, survived for a century and a half, and demonstrated that public debate and disagreement were not incompatible with effective policy or decisive collective action. Moreover, its atmosphere of open enquiry and discussion led to a unique flowering of art, drama, literature, philosophy and the sciences.

A second exemplary feature of Athenian democracy was the robust defence its supporters provided for the principle that poor citizens were every bit as capable as the well-to-do of deliberating and voting on issues of public policy. 'We give no special power to wealth,' says the Athenian in one of Euripides' plays: 'the poor man's voice commands equal authority.' 'No one,' says Pericles in the famous funeral speech at the end of the first year of the war with Sparta, 'so long as he has it in him to be of service to the city, is kept in political obscurity because of poverty.'

Aristocrats and élitists then and ever since have regarded this principle as scandalous, even politically ruinous. Only the few can know what is really good for society. The philosopher Plato likened democracy to a ship in which an inexperienced crew had seized the helm from the ship's captain, and consumed all the supplies in a drunken orgy while the ship drifted onto the rocks. In his view only philosophers, who had experienced long years of education in the knowledge of what was good for man and society, were fit rulers of a city. Democracy's supporters responded with the argument that a capacity for moral awareness and recognition of the public interest were common to all citizens as members of society, and were not the subject of any special expertise. Experts might be required for special public tasks – shipwrights, architects, engineers, etc. – but it was for the citizens themselves to decide whether and when these should be carried out. 'The cobbler makes the shoe, but only the wearer can tell where it pinches' sums up this view.

There was another argument in support of democracy, which was developed much further in modern times. Even if the special few could know what was in other people's interests better than they did themselves (which they couldn't), what incentive could they possibly have to pursue it, rather than their own interests? They might start by trying to do so, but their efforts would inevitably degenerate under the corrupting influence of power. So there was a protective argument for democracy – protecting people against the corrupting effects of power on the few – to add to the positive argument, that only by empowering the people to take their own decisions could the public good be realised.

direct and representative democracy

A confidence in ordinary people's capacity to take reasoned decisions about their own lives and, by extension, the life of the communities in which they live has always formed the bedrock of democratic thinking. However, the classical Athenian practice of giving every citizen the right to take part in public decisions in person was only possible because of the relatively small size of the city-state, which allowed its citizens to assemble together in one place. The size of the modern state makes this simply impractical, and today we think of democracy as a system of government in which citizens elect political representatives to a local or national assembly to take decisions on policy and legislation on their behalf: this is called 'representative' rather than 'direct' democracy.

Is such a system really democratic? Is it not just another example of rule by the few over the rest of society, i.e. a form of oligarchy, in which a powerful group takes decisions for everyone else? Many of the protagonists of modern representative government, from the time of the US revolution in the eighteenth century onwards, have seen the signal advantage of a representative system to lie in the fact that it is not really 'democratic': that elected representatives, typically persons of superior judgement, are able to arrive at decisions on law and policy independently of the pressures of popular opinion.

So James Madison, in the US *Federalist Papers*, wrote that, by delegating government to a small number of citizens 'whose wisdom may best discern the true interest of their country … the public voice, pronounced by the representatives of the people, will be more consonant to the public good than if pronounced by the people themselves.' And Edmund Burke, addressing the electors of Bristol who had just voted him to Parliament, insisted that it was the task of an elected representative to decide national issues as he thought best, not as the opinion of his constituents might direct. 'Your representative', he said in a famous passage, 'owes you, not his industry only, but his judgement; and he betrays, instead of serving you, if he sacrifices it to your opinion.' The logical counterpart to this assertion was that electors should be content 'to be governed by the superior wisdom of representatives', as J.S. Mill put it in his classic mid-nineteenth-century work on representative government. Or, as expressed even more forcibly by Joseph Schumpeter in the

Schumpeter

mid-twentieth century, the voters 'must understand that, once
they have elected an individual, political action is his business and
not theirs'.

These accounts of representative government do not sound
particularly democratic, since they seem to reject the basic principle
that everyone is equally entitled to express their opinion and have it
considered. What differentiates our representatives from the rest
of us is not that they have some superior qualities which others do
not possess, but that they are given the necessary *time* to deliberate
and decide public issues in our place and on our behalf. But in
a democracy they still have to listen to and take notice of the
rest of us.

This is only one of the many features that distinguish a system of
representative democracy from an oligarchy, or 'rule by the few'. It
will be useful to set out what these major differences are. Under a
democracy:

- Any citizen can in principle stand for elective office, as opposed to
  office being restricted to those with special qualifications or
  attributes.
- Key public office holders are elected by universal and equal suffrage, as opposed to being appointed.
- There is freedom of expression and a pluralism of independent
  media, contributing to energetic public debate, as opposed to
  officially controlled media with censorship restrictions.
- There is public access to official information about what government is doing, and a variety of sources of independent expertise
  as a check on government, as opposed to government secrecy and
  monopolisation of information.
- Citizens are free as of right to organise themselves and further
  their interests and values in a variety of associations, as opposed
  to this being a privilege which can be withdrawn at will.
- There are many different channels through which electors can
  seek to make their views known to their representatives, and seek
  to influence them, as opposed to communication simply being
  from the top downwards.
- Citizens have the right to vote directly on constitutional changes
  affecting their powers and those of their representatives, as
  opposed to constitutional changes being determined by others.
- All these rights are legally guaranteed, and the law is enforced by
  judges who are independent of the government of the day.

These differences are summarised in the accompanying box:

DEMOCRACY	OLIGARCHY
Public office open to all.	Office restricted to those with special attributes or qualifications.
Selection for office by election.	Selection for office by appointment.
Freedom of expression and media.	Censorship and controlled media.
Access to official information.	Public office protected by secrecy.
Free associational life.	Association a privilege.
Channels of upward influence.	Communication only downwards.
Direct vote on constitutional change.	Constitutional change decided by élite.
Rights enforced by independent judges.	Judges subordinate to the government.

Now it may well be that not all the features in the left-hand column are fully realised in democracies as we experience them, and this will be a subject for later chapters. Representative democracies often show oligarchic tendencies. Yet in principle there is a radical difference between the two types of regime. And it should be clear from this contrast that what distinguishes representative democracy from oligarchy is not just how office holders are selected, or who may stand for public office. It is also that representative democracies depend upon a continuously active citizen body if they are to function in a *democratic* way. This means that we should not pose too sharp an antithesis between representative and direct democracy. For representative government to be genuinely democratic, it requires a continual input of direct democracy on the part of active and concerned citizens.

collective action and individual choice

The contrast that I have been making can be illustrated by comparing the sphere of government and politics in a democracy with that of economic companies and businesses. These are typically oligarchies, and their system of governance has all the attributes of the right-hand column in the box above. Admittedly, elements of democracy appear, but usually only at the margin. So-called shareholder democracy is largely a sham, since it is dominated by a handful of investment funds, and the influence of workers through trade unions is narrowly circumscribed and typically accepted on sufferance. In the economic sphere, however, a system of oligarchy is usually seen as an advantage: it makes for economic efficiency, and follows naturally from the institution of private ownership. The wider accountability of businesses to society is in principle secured by two mechanisms: through a system of regulation enacted and enforced by government, and by their responsiveness to consumer demand in a competitive market-place. Companies that fail to provide the consumer with what he or she demands will not stay in business for long.

Some people call the power of consumer demand 'consumer democracy'. It is certainly a form of power, but to call it 'democracy' is a misnomer. Not only is it characterised by enormous *inequalities of wealth and spending* power, whereas the democratic principle is that of political equality, but, more importantly, the decisions on which that power is based are *individual* and *private*, rather than *collective* and *public* ones.

Here we return to a basic distinction between individual and collective decision making, which was raised at the outset. The distinction is central to understanding what democracy is about. Collective decisions are decisions taken for a group, association, or society as a whole. Since there is usually disagreement about what the best decision is, they typically involve discussion, argument and the demand for evidence, and they need an agreed method for reaching these decisions. The power of members in a democracy is twofold: that of *voting*, either directly on matters for decision, or to choose the decision makers; and that of *voice*, of contributing to and influencing the discussion. And this usually requires joining with like-minded others to make your voice and vote more effective than it would be on its own.

Consumer decisions, by contrast, are typically individual ones, and the power they involve is what is called the power of 'exit' rather than 'voice': if you are not satisfied with what you have bought, you withdraw your custom, buy a different brand, or shop somewhere else. Cumulatively, it is true, the sum of individual decisions may produce a *collective outcome*, in increasing or declining sales and profits for a company, or even the collapse of its business. But this is not the result of a conscious public process of collective decision making, involving discussion and argument. Even the act of voting for a representative, which has sometimes been likened to an individual and private choice between different products in the political market-place, takes place in the context of fierce public debate and the purposive association of like-minded citizens to influence the outcome.

It is these that are the characteristic features of democracy. At the governmental level, most of us do not have the opportunity of 'exit'. We cannot, in practice, emigrate, and even though we may choose the precise locality where we live in our country, once we have chosen we are necessarily subject to the government of that locality. We cannot avoid its taxes, or the effects of its decisions. So what power do we have if, say, a planning decision is coming up which will reduce the area of open recreational space in our neighbourhood, or allow an inappropriate multi-storey building in our residential street? We can lobby our elected councillor, mobilise our neigh-bours, join a local residents' or civic association, contact the local press, organise a demonstration at the local planning office, and so on. These are the typical democratic powers of voice and, ultimately, vote, in association with like-minded others – powers which can be used positively, to campaign for some new local facility, as well as obstructively.

Of course, these activities take time. So does the time we take in shopping. In comparison with shopping, however, the outcome is more uncertain. It is in the nature of collective decisions that they involve compromise with the views and interests of others, and that we can rarely get everything we want, even if we make our voices heard. This may seem like a big disadvantage in comparison with individual decisions, where our personal preferences reign supreme and we are accountable only to ourselves. However, decisions affecting whole groups of people are an inescapable feature of social life, and they determine the context and the limits within which our individual choices are set. The central issue of democracy is who is involved in these decisions, and how they come to be taken.

It is especially important to insist on this collective dimension of democracy, because we live in an age when maximising the freedom of individual choice has become an almost self-evident goal of public policy, and has become equated with democracy itself.

Freedom to choose is the contemporary mantra: to choose what cars
to buy and when and where to drive them, which exotic places to go
to on holiday, which schools our children should attend, which hospitals we should choose for treatment when we are ill, and so on. Yet
the sum of these individual choices has collective consequences,
sometimes quite damaging ones. Unrestricted use of cars causes
gridlock on the roads and renders public transport uneconomic.
Unlimited choice of air travel is a major contributor to global
warming. Individual choice in health and education means that
some schools and hospitals become oversubscribed, while others
enter a downward spiral of deterioration and inadequate resourcing.
At some point these consequences have to be addressed directly and
made the subject of public discussion and decision. It is then that
democracy comes into play.

In conclusion, then, democracy belongs to the sphere of collective and public decisions, rather than individual and private ones. It
is based on: the principle of equality between members and equal
citizenship; full information and free discussion on all issues for
collective decision; the citizen powers of voice and vote in association with others; and the right to stand for key elective office, and to
hold elected representatives accountable for their decisions. We
could call these for short the principles of *popular control* of public
decision making and decision makers, and *political equality*. They
are equally applicable to a small local association and to the government of a large state.

Let us then review the definitions of democracy with which we
began, in the light of these two principles. Some of the definitions
only address one of our principles (rule of the people, equal citizenship rights); some concentrate only on the freedom aspect of
democracy (civil and political liberties); some refer to the institutions through which these principles are realised (multi-partyism, a
civil society); some equate democracy with one of its social
conditions (a free-market economy), or one of its outcomes (the
well-being of the people); some give democracy an oligarchic twist
(élite competition for the people's vote), and some have little to do
with democracy at all (the end of history, etc.). Our principles can
thus give us a guide through the maze of competing definitions
which will otherwise confuse us, or lead us to believe, erroneously,
that one person's definition is as good as any other's.

Although starting with basic principles is the best way to reach a
coherent definition of democracy, however, we need to go on to

consider the institutional arrangements through which these
principles can be realised at the level of the national state. This will
form the subject of the following chapter.

further reading

Arblaster, Anthony. *Democracy*. Milton Keynes: Open University
Press, 1987.

Beetham, David and Kevin Boyle. *Introducing Democracy: 80
Questions and Answers*. Cambridge and Paris: Polity Press and
UNESCO Publishing, 1995.

Blaug, Ricardo and John Schwarzmantel, eds. *Democracy: A Reader*.
Edinburgh: Edinburgh University Press, 2001 (contains extracts
from all the classic texts cited in this chapter).

Crick, Bernard. *Democracy: A Very Short Introduction*. Oxford and
New York: Oxford University Press, 2002.

Dahl, Robert. *Democracy and its Critics*. New Haven and London:
Yale University Press, 1989.

Dahl, Robert. *On Democracy*. New Haven and London: Yale
University Press, 1998.

Saward, Michael. *Democracy*. Cambridge: Polity Press, 2003.

democratic ideas in practice

In the Introduction I suggested that democracy can best be understood as a set of ideas or principles governing how collective decisions should be made. These are the ideas of: open discussion between competing views; the equal right of members to have a say, to elect office holders from among them and to influence their deliberations; the freedom to associate with others so that the influence of vote and voice can be made more effective. In this chapter we shall look more closely at the practical arrangements which have been developed over generations to give effect to these ideas at the level of a whole society's government. I shall consider three different aspects of these arrangements: a framework of citizen rights; institutions of representative and accountable government; and the associations of what is called 'civil society' and their relation to government.

citizen rights

The starting-point of democratic government is with the citizen – that is, with you and me. It is from us that members of a government acquire their jobs and the tax revenues to perform their work on our behalf. It is to us that they are continually looking for endorsement of their actions and policies, and to us that they are at the end of the day accountable. But this only happens because as citizens we have certain rights which do not depend on the government of the day,

12

and which cannot be taken away by them. These rights should be seen as the foundation of democracy. They are the rights of free expression and enquiry, of free association and communication with others, of public assembly, and of course the right to elect a parliament and government and know what they are doing in our name. Underpinning all of these is the right to security of our person and possessions, so that these cannot be threatened, harmed or seized by government except through due legal process.

Nowadays, those of us who live in the 'old' democracies take these rights for granted. Yet they are not realised or respected everywhere in the world today, and they did not exist in previous centuries, even in Western societies. They are the result of struggles of the common people, often at considerable cost to themselves, to limit the power of oligarchic and oppressive regimes, and to make government more publicly accountable and responsive to the whole community. We cannot fully appreciate the significance of these rights without understanding something about the history of the struggles that led to their establishment, and the kind of threats to personal freedom and well-being against which they were seen to provide a much-needed protection.

the struggle against oppressive government

What were these struggles? We could distinguish three phases of popular struggle for democracy in modern Europe and America, though they often overlapped. One set of struggles was to limit the abuses of aristocratic and monarchical governments, and make them more representative and accountable to a wider public. Typical abuses were those of arbitrary arrest, detention without trial, torture in detention, confiscation of property, forcible taxation, censorship, the seizure of offending publications, government by decree rather than a proper law-making process. These have been the measures used by oppressive regimes throughout history against political opponents and anyone expressing subversive ideas. And it was the determination never to experience them again that led to the US *Bill of Rights* and the *Declaration of the Rights of Man* in France after the revolution in 1789. These lists of rights conform closely to the catalogue of abuses against which their authors were seeking protection (see extracts in box, p. 14). They also form a central component of contemporary human rights conventions, such as the International Covenant on Civil and Political Rights and the

European Convention on Human Rights (though with the masculine 'man' replaced by the gender-neutral 'person' in these texts).

the struggle for equal citizenship

So, one set of struggles over rights in Europe and America took place to protect personal and political freedoms against oppressive government. A second set of struggles was to make citizenship more inclusive of the population as a whole, and in particular to extend the right to vote and stand for public office beyond the preserve of a relatively small number of male property owners. The justification for a property qualification broke down during the nineteenth century under popular pressure as more people became subject to direct taxation, and primary education became extended more widely. And the exclusion of women gave way under the pressure of women's campaigning and also the experience of the First World War, which

---

EXTRACTS FROM THE DECLARATION OF THE RIGHTS OF MAN

VI. The law is an expression of the will of the community. All citizens have a right to concur, either personally, or by their representatives, in its formation.

VII. No man should be accused, arrested, or held in confinement, except in cases determined by the law, and according to the forms which it has prescribed.

IX. Every man being presumed innocent till he has been convicted, whenever his detention becomes indispensable, all rigour to him, more than is necessary to secure his person, ought to be provided against by the law.

XI. The unrestrained communication of thoughts and opinions being one of the most precious rights of man, every citizen may speak, write and publish freely, provided he is responsible for the abuse of this liberty in cases determined by the law.

XIV. Every citizen has a right, either by himself or his representative, to a free voice in determining the necessity of public contributions, the appropriation of them, and their amount, mode of assessment, and duration.

XV. Every community has a right to demand of all its agents, an account of their conduct.

demonstrated that women were as capable as men of performing a wide range of civilian jobs and contributing to a national war effort. Table 2.1 shows the dates when women first achieved the vote in a range of countries.

These campaigns for the extension of full citizenship rights to the whole adult population were fought under the democratic principle of equality: the equal value of each person, and their equal potential for contributing to public affairs. The old aristocratic societies of Europe had been based on the principle that a person's capacities and social position were determined by birth, so women were 'naturally' qualified for domestic duties only, blacks for slavery and a

Table 2.1 Extending the vote to women

1893	New Zealand
1902	Australia*
1906	Finland
1913	Norway
1915	Denmark, Iceland*
1917	Canada*
1918	Austria, Germany, Hungary, Ireland*, Poland, Russia, United Kingdom*
1919	Belgium, Luxembourg, Netherlands, Sweden*
1920	Czechoslovakia, United States of America
1930	South Africa (Whites), Turkey
1944	France
1945	Italy, Japan
1947	Argentina, Pakistan
1950	India
1952	Greece, Lebanon
1963	Afghanistan, Congo, Iran, Kenya, Morocco
1971	Switzerland
1984	Liechtenstein, South Africa ('Coloureds' & 'Indians')
1994	South Africa ('Blacks')

Source: Inter-Parliamentary Union *Women in National Parliaments*, http://www.ipu.org. Accessed April 2004.
* Denotes suffrage subject to conditions or restrictions

labourer's sons for similarly menial tasks. Although a few exceptions
had always been tolerated, it took the revolutionary ideas and social
changes of the eighteenth century to demonstrate that the supposedly *innate* characteristics of different social groups were the
product of social conditioning and opportunity, not the product of
'nature' itself. Of course, differences between social groups – of culture, belief, lifestyle and so on – will always remain, and their diversity is to be welcomed. But the democratic principle of equality
holds that, whatever the differences between us, there are certain
common needs and capacities which we all share, and on the basis of
which we are entitled to the same rights of citizenship.

It is one thing, however, for people to have the formal or legal
rights of equal citizenship, another for them to be able to exercise
them effectively. It was not until the civil rights campaigns of the
1960s that Blacks in the southern states of the USA were able to
attain equality of citizenship with their white compatriots. And
even today, it is still more difficult for them to achieve elective
public office, as their respective proportions in Congress compared
with their proportion in the population at large demonstrates
(see table 2.2).

Table 2.2   Representation of race in the US Congress

	Percentage population (2005 projected) [a]	Percentage representation in House of Representatives [b]	Percentage representation in Senate [b]
White	70	87	97
Black	12	9	0
Hispanic	13	4	0
Asian	4	1	2
American Indian	1	0	1

Sources:
[a] US Census Bureau 1996 *Population Projections of the United States by Age,
Sex, Race, and Hispanic Origin: 1995 to 2050*, http://www.census.gov. Accessed
April 2004.
[b] This Nation [website], http://www.thisnation.com. Accessed April 2004. Status as at
7 February 2000.

Similarly, almost everywhere, women find it more difficult than men to be selected to stand for elective office, even though they formally have the equal right to do so. Table 2.3 shows the proportion of women legislators in selected countries. A comparison of the figures for the Welsh Assembly and Scottish Parliament with the figure for the UK Parliament suggests some of the factors that might contribute to increased women's representation. Those assemblies are new, so there were no incumbent males who might resist their displacement. And special measures were taken by some of the political parties, such as twinning constituencies so that equal numbers of male and female candidates were presented to the electorate.

The example just given demonstrates that the struggle for equal citizenship is never fully complete. This applies not just to voting or the right to stand for election. It applies wherever there are groups in society who continue to experience systematic discrimination or disadvantage because of their distinctive characteristics: in their access to employment or promotion; as clients of the public services, or in their treatment at the hands of the police or other law enforcement agencies (see, for example, table 2.4). The idea that difference connotes inferiority, or presents some kind of threat, is extraordinarily persistent, and it is one that democratic societies, founded as they are on the principle of equal citizenship, continually have to combat.

the struggle for economic and social rights

A third series of popular struggles has occurred around the demand for economic and social rights as an element in citizenship. Even as early as the eighteenth century, one version of the *Declaration of the Rights of Man* contained a clause, never implemented, to the effect that 'society has a duty to ensure the sustenance of the poor either by providing them with work, or by giving the means of livelihood to those who are unable to work'. But it was the experience of the insecurities and exploitative working conditions of the Industrial Revolution from the nineteenth century onwards that fuelled widespread demands for economic and social rights: for the right of workers to join trade unions and act collectively to improve conditions; for insurance against sickness and unemployment; for access to education, medical care and affordable housing. And it was not until the middle of the twentieth century that these rights became generally realised across the industrialised world, and incorporated in the UN Declaration of Human Rights.

Table 2.3   Proportion of women in the lower house (or unicameral chamber, if appropriate) in selected countries following most recent election (1999–2003)

Country	Date of general election	Seats	Women	% women
Wales	06 2003	60	30	50.0
Rwanda	09 2003	80	39	48.8
Sweden	09 2002	349	158	45.3
Scotland	06 2003	129	51	39.5
Denmark	11 2001	179	68	38.0
Finland	03 2003	200	75	37.5
Netherlands	01 2003	150	55	36.7
Norway	09 2001	165	60	36.4
Austria	11 2002	183	62	33.9
Germany	09 2002	603	194	32.2
Argentina	10 2001	257	79	30.7
South Africa	06 1999	399	119	29.8
New Zealand	07 2002	120	34	28.3
Spain	03 2000	350	99	28.3
Vietnam	05 2002	498	136	27.3
Australia	11 2001	150	38	25.3
Switzerland	10 2003	200	50	25.0
Uganda	06 2001	304	75	24.7
Mexico	07 2003	500	113	22.6
Pakistan	10 2002	342	74	21.6
Poland	09 2001	460	93	20.2
Slovakia	09 2002	150	29	19.3
Portugal	03 2002	230	44	19.1
United Kingdom	06 2001	659	118	17.9
United States of America	11 2002	435	62	14.3
Ireland	05 2002	166	22	13.3
France	06 2002	574	70	12.2
Italy	05 2001	618	71	11.5
Romania	11 2000	345	37	10.7
Japan	11 2003	480	34	7.1

Source: Inter-Parliamentary Union *Women in National Parliaments*, http://www.ipu.org. Accessed April 2004.

Table 2.4   Racial disadvantage in the USA

		Percentage of population (2005 projected)[1]	Sentenced prisoners per 100,000 of group (1997)[2]	Percentage of population under correctional supervision[2]	Poverty incidence (percentage of group)[3]
USA		100	440	2.8	10.6
	White	70	189	2.0	8.0
	Black	12	1743	9.0	24.1
	Hispanic	13	738	–	21.8
	Asian	4	–	1.3	–
	American Indian	1	–	–	–

Sources:
1. US Census Bureau 1996 *Population Projections of the United States by Age, Sex, Race, and Hispanic Origin: 1995 to 2050*, http://www.census.gov. Accessed April 2004.
2. US Dept of Justice: Office of Justice Programs: Bureau of Justice Statistics 2000 *Correctional Populations in the United States, 1997*, November 2000, NCJ 177613 from http://www.ojp.usdoj.gov. Accessed April 2004.
3. US Census Bureau 2002 *Poverty 2002*, http://www.census.gov. Accessed April 2004.

What has the guarantee of these rights to do with democracy? It should be self-evident that we cannot play any part as citizens in the affairs of our community, or in public affairs more widely, if we lack basic education, health or a means of livelihood. What is today known as 'social exclusion' – the lack of basic amenities that most of society takes for granted – is associated closely with political exclusion – ignorance of one's rights, political apathy, failure to register for elections or to vote, an inability to make any contribution to one's community.

It does not follow from this connection that equality of citizenship requires full *economic* equality. That is an unattainable and, many would say, an undesirable goal. What it does require is that society should guarantee a minimum platform of economic and social conditions and opportunities which no one should be deprived of. And that this platform is as essential a feature of democratic citizenship as the rights to free expression and association, to stand for election and so on, since it is a necessary precondition for being able to exercise them effectively.

These three overlapping phases of popular struggle over two centuries or more have passed down to us the key elements of our rights as democratic citizens: the defence of personal and political freedoms against arbitrary and oppressive government; the right of all to participate in public affairs and to equality of treatment in public life; and the guarantee of an economic and social minimum as a condition for the exercise of other rights. In the 'old' democracies we take all these rights for granted, but we only have them because of the struggles and campaigns of our predecessors; they were not handed down from on high. Moreover, these struggles and campaigns from the past carry an important democratic lesson for the present. Those with power and advantage never give any of it up voluntarily, but only as a result of pressure from below. And that pressure is still needed if our rights are to continue to be protected and made more secure in practice.

some problems about democratic rights

At this point my account may well have left the reader with several questions about democratic rights which I have so far skated over. So let me take a few of them to further the discussion.

First, if many of our rights were designed to protect us against the abuse of state power, as I have argued, how can we also look to the state to act as their guarantor? Isn't this contradictory? The answer lies in the fact that the democratic 'state' is not a single monolithic entity, but comprises a number of separate institutions which can act to check one another. In particular, it is the task of the courts (and the judges) to ensure that the government and its officials observe the law and do not exceed their legal powers in the treatment of citizens. Any individual can appeal to the courts for legal redress if their rights have been infringed by government officials, whether by acts of commission or omission. And to make it clear what basic rights citizens have, almost all democratic systems of government have a legally binding 'bill of rights' which spells out what citizens' rights are, under what conditions they may be legally limited, and what protection citizens can expect for them. In the USA the bill of rights is formed by the first ten amendments to the constitution; in the UK, by the European Convention on Human Rights, which was incorporated into UK law only as recently as 2001. In most other countries, the bill of rights forms part of a written constitution.

Now the defence of citizens' basic rights by the courts can only be effective if the courts and their judges are fully independent of the government of the day, and refuse to be pressured or bribed by them. And this brings us to a second question which is often asked: is it democratic for non-elected judges to oppose the wishes of a popularly elected government? Is this not a denial of the democratic principle that the 'will of the majority' should prevail?

In answer, it should be said that not everything a democratically elected government does is necessarily democratic, and especially not if it infringes the basic rights of citizens. This can easily happen to an unpopular minority, or as a response to some short-term media scare or public hysteria. In relatively recent democracies the rights of opposition parties and their members are often infringed by governments which claim that their activities endanger 'public order' or 'national security'. It is in such circumstances that the role of independent courts in upholding citizens' basic rights is especially important. That doing so is itself 'democratic' has been well expressed by the US legal philosopher, Ronald Dworkin:

> True democracy is not just statistical democracy, in which anything a majority or plurality wants is legitimate for that reason, but communal democracy, in which majority decision is legitimate only if it is a majority within a community of equals. That means ... that each individual person must be guaranteed fundamental civil and political rights no combination of other citizens can take away, no matter how numerous they are or how much they despise his or her race or morals or way of life. That view of what democracy means is at the heart of all the charters of human rights.

I shall consider the idea of majority rule more fully later in this chapter. For the moment, however, this quotation may well provoke a further question. What if one person's rights conflict with another's? What if some rights in a bill of rights come into conflict with others? Freedom of expression may lead to incitement to racial or religious hatred. Freedom of assembly may lead to threats to the property, livelihood or freedom of movement of others. One of the prime responsibilities of all governments is to protect our physical security. In carrying out this responsibility, surely they are justified in curbing the rights and freedoms of potential criminals? To combat terrorism, are not governments justified in limiting even such a basic right as the right not to be imprisoned without charge or trial?

These are hugely controversial questions, and there is not the space to deal with them here. Two simple points can be made, however. In a democratic society, the presumption should always be in favour of individual freedoms, unless there is really overwhelming evidence to justify restricting them. And, secondly, such evidence should not just depend on the government's say-so, but should always be open to examination and review by the courts. Otherwise, we are in danger of losing the protections for our liberty which make democratic societies distinctive, and which previous generations have fought hard to achieve. Both of these principles have been ignored in the anti-terrorism legislation passed in the UK and USA in the aftermath of 11 September 2001.

The protection of our democratic rights, however, cannot be left to the courts alone. Their first line of defence is that they should be respected by our fellow citizens. As citizens, we not only have rights, but also corresponding responsibilities: to respect the freedom of others, and to treat them as equal citizens, especially where they differ from ourselves in their opinions, personal beliefs or lifestyle. This is not just a question of reciprocity – if I expect you to respect *my* rights, then *you* should be able to expect the same from me. Also, wherever the infringement of a person's basic rights goes unchallenged, there is a danger that it will be repeated, and that its effects will spread more widely. This gives us a good reason to support those voluntary associations that are devoted to the defence of democratic rights, such as civil liberties and human rights organisations, which work at the sharp edge in publicising and challenging serious infringements of them. These associations, and many others like them, represent a continuation of the past struggles to establish these rights in the first place, and play a vital role in their defence.

institutions of representative and accountable government

So far, I have been outlining the first of the three building blocks of representative democracy: the rights that you and I enjoy as citizens to express ourselves freely about public affairs, to join with others to achieve common purposes, and to be protected from oppressive or unduly intrusive actions by government. I come now to the second building block, the institutions of representative and accountable government. Any discussion of institutions quickly gets boring, and readers start to yawn and skip the pages, so I shall treat the next part as a kind of game: a paper-chase or thread through a maze, in which we have to find the exit or finishing post from a single starting-point; or it may turn out to be more like a game of snakes and ladders, in which we make progress only to be thrust back again towards our point of departure. In any case, the starting-point, as before, is with you and me, but now on our way to the polling-station or voting-booth, which is where the process of representative government begins.

representation in democratic government
the purpose of elections

What exactly are we doing when we cast our vote in a national election? We are doing two things: we are choosing a representative to act for us in parliament or the legislature, and we are also choosing a prime minister or president to lead the executive or government. In a presidential system (France, Russia, the USA and most countries of Latin America, Africa and Asia), these two choices are separated into two separate votes, one for the presidency and one for the members of the legislature, and may take place at different times. In a parliamentary system (the UK, most European countries and some countries of the Commonwealth), the two choices are combined into a single vote, since the parliamentary leader who can command a majority of elected members of parliament becomes the prime minister. Either way, there is an important difference between the task of government and its leadership, which is to initiate policy and give direction to public officials, and the task of parliament or legislature, which is to approve laws and expenditure, and scrutinise the actions and policies of government.

Now, compared with taking part in a mass demonstration, say, or joining a campaigning group, the act of voting may not seem very significant or empowering. Yet when combined with the votes of others it determines who obtains public office, and who is removed from it. Changes of government can be very dramatic, both for the fortunes of individuals and for the policies a country pursues. And the fact that they take place in the full glare of publicity only adds to the drama. A key test for the electoral process is how well the losers are able to face up to their rejection at the hands of the electorate. One day a person may be a premier or president with enormous power and international prestige, and the next day an ordinary citizen, with the removal vans turning up at the gates of the official residence to clear out the possessions of the rejected incumbent. A better end, you may think, than execution or banishment to run a power station in Siberia, but still a considerable shock to the self-esteem of those rejected.

Given that the stakes in an election are so high, the incentive for contestants to do everything to tilt the balance in their favour is correspondingly great. Electoral fraud has been practised in many forms ever since elections were first conducted: bribing electors, preventing them from registering to vote, threatening them, impersonating voters, disrupting meetings of opposing candidates, seizing ballot-boxes, stuffing them with your own votes, rigging the count, declaring opponents' votes invalid, and so on. Most of these forms of fraud have occurred in the past in the 'old' democracies, and at least two of them as recently as the contested presidential election of 2000 in the USA. Nowadays, most countries have appointed independent electoral commissions to ensure that the electoral process is genuinely 'free and fair', and welcome election observers from both home and abroad to give additional credibility to the results.

If the possibility of dirty tricks is closed off, however, there are other ways to tilt the electoral 'playing field' in one's favour. Rivals can simply be out-spent in the media campaign. Whole media channels can be controlled through private ownership, or through government control of state-owned media. In any case, the government in power always enjoys a certain advantage from incumbency. It monopolises public information and policy initiatives in the years and months prior to an election. In the UK, it can even choose the date of an election to maximise its chances of success.

Legislation to reduce such inequalities between candidates, e.g. by imposing limits on campaign expenditure, providing candidates with free air time on publicly owned media, and so on, can make a significant difference, but cannot eliminate all the inequalities. At best, electoral competition is a rough and ready process, and the playing field is rarely a level one. Nevertheless, when public opinion is moving strongly in one direction, it will usually prevail. If not, then we would have to conclude that the will of the people has been frustrated, and democracy itself has become a sham.

the point of political parties

Let us return to the beginning of our maze at the polling-station. You will know that when we vote, we are not only voting for an individual candidate, but for the political party which the candidate represents. Why do we need political parties? Could we not just choose the individual candidate in whom we had most confidence? In eighteenth-century parliaments and legislatures, this is typically what happened. And that meant that a fresh majority in parliament had to be cobbled together for each new piece of legislation. In this context, Edmund Burke made a good case for the advantages of political parties. It was not enough, he argued, that people should be able to express their political opinions freely. Their opinions needed to have influence, and to be given effect. And that could only happen by the like-minded joining together, preferably in semi-permanent associations organised around settled principles of policy. As he put it succinctly, 'when bad men combine, the good must associate'!

From the point of view of electors, the existence of political parties means that in choosing an individual candidate, you know that he or she is one of a group who are all committed to pursuing similar policies once they are elected. And that gives the electorate a greater degree of control over the policies as well as the personnel of government. Or, if their chosen candidate is part of an opposition minority, electors know that opposition to the government will be conducted on the basis of an alternative set of principles and policies which they support.

Naturally, there are disadvantages to all this, which are frequently commented on. There is the phenomenon of opposition for opposition's sake. And there is the unedifying spectacle of legislators being 'whipped' into line in support of policies which they do not really believe in. Here again, Burke, while advocating political parties, also had a realistic appreciation of their limits. No representative, he wrote, should 'blindly follow the opinions of party, when in direct opposition to your own clear ideas; a degree of servitude that no worthy man [sic] could bear the thought of submitting to'.

This qualification apart, if we did not have political parties, we should soon find it necessary to reinvent them, for all their current unpopularity. This is because they provide the institutional means for like-minded citizens to exercise an influence over the political process which they could not have as separate individuals. Moreover, because the degree of electoral support they enjoy is the best test of the distribution of political opinion in a country, how they are treated by the electoral system becomes important. Here, our route takes us unavoidably through the snake-pit of different types of electoral system.

electoral systems

In previous times, before the establishment of political parties, and when electors were simply choosing the best individual to represent their locality in parliament, it made good sense to have a simple constituency-based system of voting. Here, electors were divided into geographical constituencies, and the candidate with the most votes in each constituency was declared the winner, whether or not they won a majority of all the votes cast. This 'plurality' or 'first-past-the-post' system becomes problematic, however, once electors come to treat their vote as one for a national political party and its programme. Then we cannot easily ignore the arbitrary effect that a constituency-based system with a single member may have on the overall national outcome for the different parties.

Consider an extreme example. In an imaginary country we could call 'Lottoland' there are four political parties. Party A, the leftists, enjoys the national support of forty per cent of the electorate; party B, the rightists, has thirty per cent; party C, the centrists, has twenty per cent; and party D, the nationalists, has the remaining ten per cent. Now, suppose that this distribution of national party support were to be reflected in each individual constituency. Under a plurality electoral system, party A would win one hundred per cent of the seats in parliament, although on only forty per cent of the national vote; and there would be no representation for the other sixty per cent of voters. Could such a system be sustainable?

Of course, it never happens in as extreme a form as this. But under this system, everything depends on the particular degree of concentration of party support in individual constituencies. Consider the following typical result of a recent general election in the UK (table 2.5), where this system operates for elections to the Westminster Parliament.

Such an outcome means treating the votes of different electors unequally, since some will count for more than others. And the national parliament cannot be properly representative of the distribution of party support and political opinion in the country.

Table 2.5 Disproportionality in the Westminster Parliament
(June 2001)

	Percentage of vote	No. seats	Percentage of seats
Labour	40.7	413	62.7
Conservative	31.7	166	25.2
Liberal Democrat	18.3	52	7.9
Other	9.3	28	4.2

Source: BBC

It is to limit such inequities that systems of so-called 'proportional representation' have been devised. These can take different forms. One type (the single transferable vote or STV) involves multi-member constituencies, in which electors can rank candidates in order of preference. This enables supporters of smaller parties to achieve political representation, and also gives electors the opportunity to choose between candidates of the same party. It operates, for example, in Ireland. A second type allows electors in a constituency to cast two votes, one for a constituency candidate and one for a regional or national party list (mixed member system or MMS). Once the constituency candidates have been elected, the numbers from each party list to be elected are then determined so as to bring the party's overall parliamentary representation into line with its proportion of the popular vote. Again, this system allows the supporters of smaller parties to achieve some parliamentary representation, and produces a parliament that is broadly representative of political opinion in the country. It operates, for example, in Germany and New Zealand. Examples of ballot-papers from each of these types are given in figures 2.1 and 2.2.

When we talk about a legislature or parliament being 'representative', we can mean two different things. One is that it is composed of *representatives*, who act on behalf of their constituents and are accountable to them. They are, as it were, their agents in the representative assembly. The other meaning is that the assembly as a whole is *representative* of the electorate, in the sense that it reflects their key characteristics. Of these characteristics, the most

YOU HAVE TWO VOTES

PARTY VOTE	ELECTORATE VOTE
EXPLANATION	EXPLANATION
This vote decides the share of the seat which each of the parties listed below will have in Parliament. Vote by putting a tick in the box immediately after the party you choose.	This vote decides the candidate who will be elected as Member of Parliament for the Any Town constituency. Vote by putting a tick in the box immediately before the candidate you choose.

Vote for only one party	Vote here	Vote here	Vote for only one candidate
Bus	☐	☐	Diesel, Eric BUS PARTY
Boat	☐	☐	Draught, Bob BOAT PARTY
Car	☐	☐	Ford, John CAR PARTY
		☐	Goods, Sarah INDEPENDENT
Scooter	☐	☐	Kidd, Sam SCOOTER PARTY
Aeroplane	☐	☐	Pilot, Avril AEROPLANE PARTY
Bicycle	☐	☐	Raleigh, Jim BICYCLE PARTY
Tram	☐	☐	Track, Alice TRAM PARTY
Boot	☐	☐	Trainer, Dawn BOOT PARTY

Figure 2.1.   *Example of an MMP ballot-paper*

important is that it should reflect the distribution of political opinion in the country, as demonstrated in the votes for the respective political parties. This is what a system of proportional representation seeks to achieve. But a democratic assembly should also reflect politically salient *social* characteristics of the electorate, such as gender and ethnicity, so that all major social groups can recognise that they are fully included in the political process. This is the counterpart to the idea, already discussed, that there should be genuine equality of opportunity for any citizen to stand for election and become a political representative.

INSTRUCTIONS

1. See that the official mark is on the paper.
2. Mark 1 in the box beside the candidate of your first choice, mark 2 in the box beside the candidate of your second choice, and so on. You may mark as many candidates as you wish.
3. Fold the paper to conceal your vote and put it in the ballot-box.

Vote
here

Cat – Lap Lovers' Party
(Tabby Cat, of 21 High Street, Nap Town; Mouser.)

☐

Cow
(Daisy Cow, of 77 Herd Street, The Dairy; Creamer.)

☐

Dog – Kennel Party
(Fido Dog, of 1 The Street, Bone Town; Guard.)

☐

Felix – Lap Lovers' Party
(A. Felix, of 51 Sunny Street, Nap Town; Purrer.)

☐

Mongrel – Kennel Party
(Rex Mongrel, of 43 Chase Street, Kennel Town; Watchman.)

☐

Pig
(Porky Pig, of 35 Main Street, Sty; Cleaner.)

☐

Sylvester – Lap Lovers' Party
(Sly Sylvester, of 4 The Cushion, Nap Town; Cream Taster.)

☐

Figure 2.2. *Example of an STV ballot-paper*

forming a government in a parliamentary system

As with almost any aspect of democratic arrangements, there is a corresponding downside to the proportional systems of parliamentary representation that I have just discussed. This is that the choice of government rests on negotiation between parties in parliament and not on the direct choice of the electorate, since no one party is likely to win an overall majority of seats. So in our Lottoland, where the proportion of popular support for the parties would now, under a proportional election system, be precisely mirrored by their representation in parliament, a number of possible combinations of governing coalition are possible. Two, however, look most likely: a left of centre government composed of parties A and C (forty per cent plus twenty per cent); and a right of centre one, composed of parties B, C and D (thirty per cent plus twenty per cent plus ten per cent). This gives the centrist party C a crucial, and some would say, unfair level of influence, and one that might deny the largest party any place in government.

However, it usually happens in practice that, where the relative strength of the parties follows a clear shift in electoral opinion from one to another, this is then reflected in the resulting process of government formation. In any case, it is surely desirable to have a government that is supported by a clear majority of the electorate, rather than forty per cent of it, or even less. The price is an element of uncertainty, and perhaps some unseemly haggling after an election over the precise terms of collaboration between the parties that are to form the government.

A more difficult situation occurs in those countries where the political parties align themselves with relatively permanent social groupings of race, religion, language, and so on. In most countries, there are many voters who will switch from one party to another between elections, either on grounds of policy, or because of a changed assessment of their leadership or record in office. It is such shifts that produce changes in government from one election to the next, and that enable most electors to be sometimes on the winning and sometimes on the losing side. But if people vote for a party, not because of its policy, record or leadership, but as an affirmation and defence of their fixed social identity, then the relative support for the parties can remain static over time.

Consider our Lottoland again, only this time where fifty-five per cent of the electorate belongs to ethnic group Y and forty-five per cent to group Z. Because of the historic rivalry between them, political parties have formed to represent and defend each group's interests. Then one party is likely to be permanently in government, and the other permanently excluded from power, with the corresponding danger that its voters become second-class citizens in their own country, and disadvantaged in access to jobs, housing and so on. In such a situation, it may well be that, for equality of citizenship to be secured, and for both groups to feel equally included in the political process, some special measures for government formation are required. This might take the form, for example, that both groups and the parties that represent them are guaranteed a share in governmental power and positions through a power-sharing executive, or a rotating presidency. Such special schemes have long been in force in Belgium and the Lebanon, and more recently in Bosnia–Herzegovina and under the Belfast agreement in Northern Ireland.

Again, there are disadvantages to such consensual or 'consociational' arrangements. They tend to reinforce even further the idea that people are defined only by their particular social group. And they provide no opportunity for 'kicking the rascals out' and producing a change of government at the ballot-box. Yet these arrangements show that there may be circumstances where the idea of majority rule has to be modified in order to ensure the more fundamental principle of equal citizenship and equal opportunity to attain a share of governmental office. They also show how difficult it is to generalise about systems of election and government formation, in abstraction from the particular social and political conditions of each country.

government accountability

Our route through the maze, with some detours on the way, has now brought us to the point where we have a parliament or legislature chosen by the electorate, and a head of government – premier or president – also in place. In one manner or another, they can be seen to 'represent' the people as a result of the electoral process. It is now time to examine what happens when a government takes office, and what a democracy requires of it. Naturally, we expect a government to be effective: to run its large administration efficiently, and to set goals for policy that are realistic and achievable, and within the broad outlines of its election programme. Crucially also, given the enormous powers and taxpayers' money it has at its disposal, we expect a government to be publicly *accountable*.

'Accountability' is a central requirement today for anyone who wields power and authority in any kind of institution. It means, first, that they have to be able to 'give an account' of their actions and policies: to explain and justify them to an appropriate audience. It also means that there is a body or bodies which can 'hold them to account': to ensure that they act within the terms and conditions of their authority, and conform to standards of conduct that are appropriate to their office. This crucial aspect of accountability requires two main conditions in a checking body: it should have full and accurate

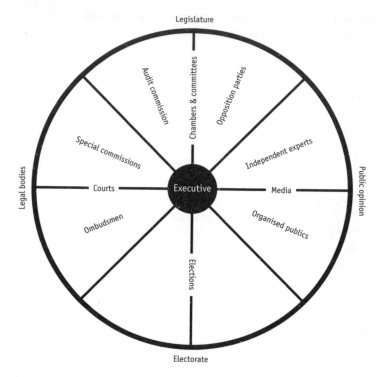

Figure 2.3. *The wheel of accountability*

information about what the office-holders are doing, and it should possess some power of *sanction* in the event that they misuse their power, or that confidence is lost in their performance. Access to information and the power of sanction are the keys to effective accountability.

Now a distinctive characteristic of a *democratic* political system is the variety of different bodies to which the government is account-able. I have set these out diagrammatically in the form of a wheel, with the government or executive as the hub and the checking bodies as the rim (see figure 2.3). I have grouped these into four main segments: the legislature or parliament, legal bodies, organs of public opinion, and the electorate itself. Each of these has its distinct-ive mode of access to information and form of sanction. In any functioning democracy, we will find that some of these bodies work more effectively than others, and that they vary in prominence as the political cycle progresses. But if any one of these segments is seriously defective, the wheel of democratic accountability will not turn. I shall describe each of them in order.

parliament or legislature

This has the most direct and explicit responsibility for holding the government to account. It has a correspondingly wide range of methods for securing information about government activity, through debates, reports, the questioning of ministers and their officials, the demand for documents, and so on, both in the full chamber and in specialist committees. It has various essentially *political* sanctions it can bring to bear, including the delay and obstruction of government business, the withholding of approval for expenditure and taxation, the censuring of ministers and their officials, or the ultimate sanction of removal from office.

Legislatures can have the greatest checking power in a presidential system when the legislature is controlled by a different party from that of the president; this can lead to so-called 'gridlock', where the president's ability to carry policy through is severely limited. Legislatures have the least ability to check the government in a parliamentary system when the governing party enjoys a large majority in parliament, and the main opposition party is not seen as a credible alternative government, as has been the case in the UK for most of the period since 1979. In all types of democratic system, opposition parties have a key role in subjecting government policy to critical scrutiny.

legal bodies

We have already considered the importance of the courts in defending citizen rights and the 'rule of law'. Their role is to ensure the accountability of government for the legality of its actions. Apart from outright criminality, they can typically only act in responsive mode, in response to cases of maladministration or abuse of power that are initiated by aggrieved individuals. Then they have strong powers of access to information through the disclosure of documents, and compulsory cross-examination of officials. And the *legal* sanctions they have available, of redress or punishment via due legal process, are also powerful ones.

Alongside the courts are special legal commissions of enquiry, both occasional and permanent. Of the latter, anti-corruption commissions are now common, and they typically have the power to initiate legal proceedings, rather than merely respond to cases brought by individuals. The most accessible legal body for the ordinary citizen, however, is the ombudsman or 'public defender', though their powers of investigation and sanction are rarely as strong as the courts. Yet because access to them is free of charge, they constitute an important avenue for complaint and redress on the part of citizens who are unable to afford the cost of litigation. And in many countries they have proved to be the public institution in which people have the greatest degree of trust and confidence, more than governments, politicians, the courts, or the police.

organs of public opinion

'Public opinion' is something rather vague and elusive, hardly an entity that seems capable of holding government to account. It may help, therefore, if we can specify some of the key agencies that contribute to forming it, and identify their different modes of access to information. Most important are the media of communication – press and broadcasting. Good journalists have the capacity to dig for information which governments prefer to hide; investigative journalism is the life-blood of democracy. And the media as a whole provide the main means for disseminating information about government, as well as shaping people's responses by the way they select and present it. Then there are the independent experts whom we see continually on our TV screens, who are able to assess for us the accuracy of the technical information on which so much government policy nowadays is based. Finally on my list are the 'organised publics': the huge army of associations representing and campaigning on behalf of different sections of society – workers, pensioners, the disabled, and so on – who have a grass-roots knowledge of how government policy is impacting on them, which they can bring to public attention.

All of these agencies which contribute to public opinion are strong on access to information about government and its policies. They are even more effective in this respect if there is strong freedom of information legislation, giving journalists and interested parties access as of right to government documents and data. Yet these agencies also appear weak in terms of any sanction they can bring to bear on government. They posses merely what the philosopher Bentham called a *moral* sanction, that of public criticism or embarrassment. Yet the force of this sanction ultimately derives from the one which is available to the public as a whole, electoral dismissal from office. And that is far from weak.

the electorate

Accountability, I have argued, involves a power of sanction in a checking body. The ultimate sanction on a government, and the one that underpins all the others, is the power of electoral dismissal. If a government has nothing to fear from facing the electorate, say because it can manipulate the electoral outcome, or because the electoral playing field is grossly slanted in its favour, then all other forms of sanction will be correspondingly weakened. What has a government to fear from a critical report in the legislature, or an embarrassing revelation in the press, or even a contempt of court ruling by a high court judge, if it knows it is secure in its prospect of re-election? *Uncertainty* of the next electoral outcome is crucial to the accountability of democratic government.

All very well, you may say, but elections only take place once every few years, and they do not seem that powerful. Yet they cast a long shadow in front of them. This is an example of what has been called the 'law of anticipated reactions'. You do not have to be continually exercising power for it to have an effect on others. This is because they will be continuously adapting their behaviour in anticipation of its possible exercise. This is how accountability works. If the electoral process is fair and robust, then governments will be continually sensitive to the impact their actions and policies will have on public opinion, with an eye to a future electoral reckoning. And it is this sensitivity that gives the other forms of sanction, in the legislature and the courts, much of their force.

Our journey has now brought us back to our starting-point, to the polling-booth; the exit from the maze proves to be in the same place as the entrance. Our exploration of representative and accountable government has taken us past different types of democratic system, presidential and parliamentary, via a detour on electoral malpractice, to political parties and their uses. We then moved through the snake-pit of different electoral systems, and the jungle of different modes of government formation, reflecting on the idea of majority rule as we went. Discovering the meaning of representation and accountability are two challenges we have had to grapple with, before the exploration of the different agencies of government accountability has brought us back to our starting-point. The journey may have been a long one, but it has been necessary if we are to understand what democratic government is about in practice.

the associational life of civil society

The institutional arrangements discussed in the previous section form only one part of democracy. Equally important is the way citizens organise themselves to run their own affairs and to meet needs and purposes they share with others – for mutual support, welfare, the running of education, sport and leisure, protection at work, improving the local environment, etc. The list is endless. The sum of this associational life has been called 'civil society'.

Why is it important for democracy? There are a number of reasons. This is where we experience democracy in action most directly: where we can ourselves engage in discussion about actions and policies for a group, and contribute to their implementation. A second reason lies in the contribution the associations of civil society make to the democratic quality of government, through helping ensure its accountability and responsiveness to citizens. Third is that the knowledge, skills and attitudes people develop through their own groups and associations carry over into and enrich the wider public sphere.

democracy in action

Democracy, as we saw in the Introduction, is about doing things with others. Where freedom of expression and association are guaranteed, people will naturally get together when there is a common need to be met: in co-operatives, clubs, societies, faith groups, charities, trade unions, self-help groups of all kinds. Some of these may be short-lived for specific purposes; others are relatively permanent features of the social and economic landscape, and have formal constitutions with a membership and elected officers.

Even where the freedoms of expression and association are tightly restricted, as under an authoritarian regime, associational life will not disappear. Indeed, in many countries it has been organisations such as churches, women's groups, trade unions, 'mothers of the disappeared', which have played a key role in accelerating the downfall of an oppressive regime. However, under such a regime, any expression of self-organisation by citizens will be tightly restricted and supervised. Under Communist regimes, in particular, almost every association had to be integrated into the Communist party hierarchy, with its party minders, and had to toe the party line. Under a democracy, by contrast, people organise themselves quite independently of government or the state, and determine their own agendas. It is precisely this independence that enables them to play a broader democratic role.

In a classic account of US democracy in the mid-nineteenth century, the French writer Tocqueville expressed his astonishment at the vigour of its associational life when compared with his native France, then under restored monarchical rule:

> No sooner do you set foot on American soil than you find yourself in a sort of tumult. All around you everything is on the move: here the people of a district are assembled to discuss the possibility of building a church … elsewhere it is the village farmers who have left their furrows to discuss the plan for a road or a school … And here is yet another gathering which regards drunkenness as the main source of ills in the state, and has come to enter into a solemn undertaking to give an example of temperance.

Tocqueville was writing at a time when the scope of government was not nearly as extensive as it is today. If public facilities were to be provided, it often had to be done by the citizens' own initiative. Yet the key point he was making was that such citizen-initiated activity was as much a part of democracy as voting for a representative or petitioning the government. And it started in the school, 'where the children, even in their games, submit to rules settled by themselves, and punish offences which they have defined themselves'. Apart from one or two exceptions I discuss below, it does not matter what the purpose of the association may be, or how seemingly trivial or non-political. If it provides the opportunity for its members to contribute to discussions about its actions, rules and policies, or to help in running it or in implementing its decisions, then it is an example of democracy in action.

There has been much recent discussion among political scientists about whether this democratic pattern of civic activism is now in serious decline, both in the US and more widely. The privatisation of leisure through television and home entertainment, so it is argued, combined with individual consumerism, has led to a broad retreat from public life, especially among the younger generation. Evidence from recent surveys in the USA and UK, however, does not seem to

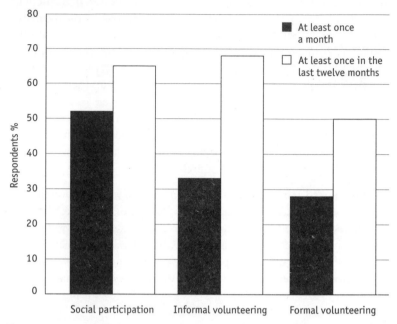

Figure 2.4. *Participation in voluntary and community activities by type of activity*

Source: Home Office, 2001 Home Office Citizenship Survey, Home Office, 2003, p. 77.

bear this out. For example, the 2001 UK Home Office survey of active participation in communities showed fifty per cent of the population regularly involved with organisations or clubs ('social participation'); while nearly a third gave time regularly in informal or organised 'volunteering', often of an extremely time-consuming character, such as fund-raising or organising meetings or events (see figure 2.4). These are not insignificant figures, nor do they bear out fears of a decline among younger age groups. Similarly, a careful examination of survey evidence in the USA suggests that membership in voluntary associations has not shown any significant decline there either, only a shift between different kinds of groups and organisations.

interacting with government

There are many ways in which, as citizens, we can engage with government between elections to express our opinions: through our elected representatives; by signing petitions; by contacting government officials or ministers directly; through the ombudsman, and so on. Often the most effective means will be in association with others, as a member of a group or organisation which represents our views or interests. This is a second aspect of the contribution of associations to democracy.

Many of the organisations we belong to may not have any explicitly political purpose – bird-watching groups, sports associations, co-operatives, charities, and so on. Yet government actions and policies will frequently impinge upon them and the interests they represent. Then they necessarily become engaged in advocacy which is explicitly political: to help bring about changes in government policy, or to respond to changes that the government itself is considering. On particularly important issues, voluntary organisations will seek to mobilise their members in a more active campaigning role, or to provide additional financial support.

Why should governments take any notice? Policy is likely to be better made if the opinions of those who may be affected by it, or who know most about it, are consulted in its formulation. Once made, it is likely to be more respected by those involved; this is particularly important where people's co-operation is required for the implementation of a policy. In any case, in most democracies, government is *required* to consult in the process of policy and legislation, and has formal mechanisms for interested parties to make representations, and for their proper consideration and response.

There are some potential drawbacks here, however. Governments are supposed to represent the electorate as a whole, not just particular or sectional interests, so there is a limit to the attention they should give to the views of special groups, however numerous their membership. Moreover, in practice, some organisations carry much greater clout by virtue of superior financial resources, or because they have always had easier access to ministers. Indeed, the experience of 'departmental capture' by special interests is not uncommon: agriculture ministries by the farmers' lobby; transport ministries by the road-building lobby; defence and foreign ministries by representatives of the arms trade, and so on.

Such inequalities of access have always been a matter of concern for those who take the principle of political equality seriously, and I will consider them more fully in the next chapter. Of more recent concern, however, is the practice of governments contracting the delivery of public services, such as housing or welfare services, to voluntary organisations in the charitable sector. While this practice may seem to be of mutual benefit, there is a danger that it can come to compromise the independence of such associations by setting their agendas from above, and blunting their advocacy role in relation to government policy. It has been calculated for the UK, for example, that around sixty per cent of funding of the voluntary sector now comes from government through various channels.

Despite these qualifications, however, it remains true that membership and participation in voluntary associations is one of the most effective ways through which the views and interests of like-minded citizens can be brought to bear upon government in an organised fashion. And if we feel that our opinions have been simply ignored, whether by government or our fellow citizens, then there is always the possibility of more short-term forms of action with others: mass demonstrations, sit-ins and other forms of public protest. Such actions, requiring as they do considerable commitment of time and effort on the part of the participants, provide an opportunity for assessing the intensity of objectors' views, rather than by simply counting heads, as in an opinion poll. As we have already seen, the battle for public opinion is one of the main arenas for democratic politics, and citizens acting together can be as much involved in this as governments.

These different forms of action show again how mistaken it can be to posit a radical contrast between 'direct' and 'representative' democracy, as many people do. Representative democracy only works in a democratic way because, in between elections, citizens involve themselves in all kinds of actions with others to influence government, which contribute to its continuing responsiveness and accountability.

qualities of the democratic citizen

A third and final democratic feature of society's associational activity is its contribution to shaping a broader culture of public involvement, and the personal characteristics appropriate to it. In almost any form of association we can learn to co-operate with others, develop organisational skills and the ability to resolve differences through discussion. Achieving results will increase people's confidence in their own effectiveness and in the value of acting together. Such attributes are likely to affect the quality of public life more generally. It is for this reason that democratic educators are keen that students should be able to participate in the governance of their class, school or college, and to be actively involved in projects in the wider community; not just learn about 'civics' as another curriculum subject.

How far do such citizen qualities really serve to sustain a democratic system of government, and how far are they themselves a product of it? Political scientists have endlessly debated this chicken-and-egg question, and never fully resolved it. Tocqueville saw the two as mutually reinforcing. The free conditions of democracy, he wrote, encourage the associational life of civil society to flourish. But the experience of that in turn makes people highly resistant to any attempts at despotism. That is probably the best that can be said on the subject.

We should be aware of some exceptions to such a generalisation, however. Not all associations contribute to democracy; some are indicative of a highly 'uncivil' society. There are illegal organisations, such as mafias, drugs cartels and other criminal associations. There are paramilitary groups or militias, vigilante bands and paedophile rings. No doubt all of these help develop their members' organisational skills and their sense of personal 'efficacy'. Yet they can be enormously damaging to the quality of public life, and may even threaten to subvert the democratic process itself.

Combating these forms of 'uncivil society' is a matter for the law enforcement agencies. More complex from a democratic point of view are those legal associations and groups whose programme or ideology is a racist one, or one that encourages the idea of supremacy of one social group over another. How to respond to these is a matter of considerable controversy. On the one side, it is argued that the freedoms of expression and association require us to allow their existence, and that, on balance, it is better to have them out in the open where their level of public support can be assessed, and where they can be openly campaigned against. On the other side, it is contended that democracies should not tolerate groups or parties which, if they ever achieved significant influence upon government, might seek to deny some sections of the population their basic democratic rights, or to subvert the democratic process

itself. It is doubtful if we can come to a definitive solution to
this question in the abstract, without knowing more about the
particular social and political circumstances in which it has become
contentious.

conclusion

This last conclusion above is one that applies to a number of the
issues considered in this chapter. In it, my purpose has been to
sketch out the main institutional features of a working democracy,
and show how they each contribute to the realisation of basic democratic ideas or principles: that the people should have the main influence or control over the decisions that affect their lives, and do so in
conditions of political equality. We have seen how the three building
blocks of the democratic process of government work together to
this end: the framework of basic citizen rights, the institutions of
representative and accountable government, and the associational
life of civil society.

Yet we have also seen how all these elements may at certain points
involve having to strike a balance between conflicting pressures or
imperatives. Different rights may conflict with one another. A focus
on accountability to the exclusion of all else may produce governmental gridlock. Systems of proportional representation may
enhance equality between voters, but reduce the electorate's control
over the choice of government. Civil and political freedoms may
make security more difficult in an insecure world. Enhancing the
responsiveness of government may give advantage to groups with
superior financial and organisational resources. And so on.
Although it is possible to identify these points of tension in general
terms, where precisely the balance should be struck will depend
upon the individual circumstances of a given country. And how they
are to be resolved will itself be a major subject for a country's
ongoing democratic debate.

further reading

Axtmann, Roland, ed. *Understanding Democratic Politics*. London
and Thousand Oaks CA: Sage Publications, 2003.

Beetham, David, Iain Byrne, Pauline Ngan and Stuart Wier.
Democracy under Blair. London: Politicos, 2002.

Bobbio, Norberto. *The Age of Rights*. Cambridge: Polity Press, 1996.

Catt, Helena. *Democracy in Practice*. London and New York:
Routledge, 1999.

Dahl, Robert. *How Democratic is the American Constitution?*
New Haven and London: Yale University Press, 2002.

Dworkin, Ronald. *A Bill of Rights for Britain*. London: Chatto and
Windus, 1990.

Kaviraj, Sudipta and Sunil Khilnani, eds. *Civil Society: History and
Possibilities*. Cambridge: Cambridge University Press, 2001.

Lijphart, Arend. *Democracies: Patterns of Majoritarian and
Consensus Government in Twenty-one Countries*. New Haven and
London: Yale University Press, 1984.

Miroff, Bruce, Raymond Seidelman and Todd Swanstrom.
The Democratic Debate: An Introduction to American Politics.
Boston and New York: Houghton Mifflin, 1998.

Phillips, Anne. *Engendering Democracy*. Cambridge: Polity Press,
1991.

de Tocqueville, Alexis. *Democracy in America*. New York: Alfred
Knopf, 1945.

Ware, Alan. *Citizens, Parties and the State*. Cambridge: Polity Press,
1987.

sources of disillusion in the 'old' democracies

In chapter 1 I set out the basic ideas or principles of democracy, and in chapter 2 I showed how these ideas are realised in practice through the institutional arrangements of a representative democracy. My presentation in both chapters has been positive and 'upbeat': how democracies at best can and should work. It is now time to take a much harder look at how democracies actually perform in practice. Why is it that, just when the idea of democracy has become widely accepted around the world, so many people have also become disillusioned with it? In this chapter I shall examine the sources of disillusion or disaffection in the 'old' democracies of West and Northern Europe, North America and Australia/New Zealand. In the next chapter I shall look at the successes and setbacks of democratisation in the 'new and emerging' democracies of Latin America, Africa, Asia and the rest of Europe.

When we talk about disillusion with democracy in the 'old' democracies, we need to be clear what we are referring to. It is not disillusion with the *idea* of democracy. Nor does it represent a declining interest in politics, or in people's readiness to organise and mobilise through groups and associations in civil society. As we have already seen, this last remains remarkably vigorous. What 'disillusion' refers to is a marked decline in confidence in government and the representative processes of democracy, which in the previous chapter I called the 'institutions of representative and accountable government'.

Although there are variations between the countries I have grouped together above, the evidence indicates a general pattern of declining public confidence in these institutions over the past fifteen years, and in some cases much longer. The evidence comes from three sources. First, public opinion surveys demonstrate 'a general erosion in support for politicians and political institutions in most advanced industrial democracies'. In the case of the USA, this erosion goes back a long way: whereas in 1966 forty-one per cent of the population had 'a great deal of confidence' in the presidency, and forty-two per cent in Congress, by 1996 these figures had fallen to thirteen per cent and five per cent respectively.

A second source of evidence comes from declining voter turnouts in national elections. In the USA, these have rarely risen above fifty per cent in any case. But the older democracies in general have seen a clear decline over time, as table 3.1 shows. A third source of evidence comes from the decline in membership of political parties. In the UK, for example, party membership has halved over the past twenty years. As we saw in the previous chapter, elections and political parties constitute key elements of representative democracy. If they attract increasingly fewer people to participate in them, this must be taken as a significant warning sign.

Taken together, these different kinds of evidence reveal increasing dissatisfaction with governments, politicians and the representative process. What is the explanation for this? In theory, the cause might lie with the *voters*. For example, increasing consumer sophistication among voters might lead them to have higher standards of expectation of government and public services than previously, even though government performance had not changed. Most commentators, however, take the view that the problem lies primarily with government itself, and with changes that have taken place in the conditions of government and politics over the past fifteen years or so.

I share this conclusion. In this chapter, I shall explore three different trends that have been evident in government over the recent period, which I shall call a decline in *autonomy*, a decline in *capacity* and a decline in *credibility*, respectively. Together, these help explain the increased level of dissatisfaction on the part of voters. Each of the three also serves to highlight a key problem or dilemma in the condition of democracy today.

decline in government autonomy

What I describe as a decline in the autonomy of government is a decrease in governments' ability to determine policy in the public

Table 3.1   Electoral turnout in selected European democracies, 1980 to 2000*

Percentage turnout of registered voters

	Austria	Belgium	Finland	France	Germany	Greece	Ireland	Italy
1980	92.2	94.6	75.3	70.9	88.6	81.5	76.2	90.4
1985	90.5	93.6	72.1	78.5	84.3	83.8	73.3	89.0
1990	86.1	92.7	68.4	66.2	77.8	84.5	68.5	87.4
1995	86.0	91.2	68.6	68.9	79.0	76.3	66.1	86.1
2000	80.4	90.6	65.3	60.3	82.2	75.0	62.6	81.4

	Holland	Norway	Portugal	Spain	Sweden	Switzerland	UK
1980	87.0	82.0	85.5	68.1	90.7	48.1	76.0
1985	85.8	84.0	75.4	70.4	89.9	48.9	72.8
1990	80.3	83.2	68.2	70.0	86.7	46.0	77.8
1995	78.8	75.9	66.3	78.1	88.1	42.3	71.5
2000	73.2	75.0	61.1	68.7	80.1	43.2	59.4

Source: International IDEA 2004 *Voter turnout since 1945*, http://www.idea.int. Accessed April 2004.

* Data shown is for the nearest election to each of the index years. Where more than five elections have taken place between 1980 and 2000 some results have been excluded.

interest because of their subordination to the requirements of domestic business interests. A degree of subordination of government to business interests has always been a feature of representative democracies in a market economy, or 'market democracies' as they have been called. In a classic study written in 1977 by Charles Lindblom entitled *Politics and Markets*, the author detailed a number of different factors explaining business influence over government policy. Most basic is the fact that, in a market economy, economic activity is not directly under the control of government, but depends upon private business decisions for investment, production and the delivery of employment and services. This means that a government's goals for the economy, which lie at the heart of all government policy, can only be met *indirectly*, through securing conditions favourable to business, and giving priority to its interests.

There may be nothing particularly sinister in this, says Lindblom; it is simply a fact of life in a market economy, which provides the setting for all contemporary democracies. However, this inherent bias of government towards business is reinforced by other political advantages that business has, when compared, say, with other associations that try to influence government. It has far superior resources of wealth and organisation to conduct effective lobbying of government, or the persuasion of public opinion. Above all, it has attained an insider position in many government ministries, where it acts as a privileged consultant and provider of necessary information in the formation of policy. Because of their key function in the economy, he writes, 'businessmen cannot be left knocking at the doors of the political systems, they must be invited in'.

Lindblom concludes that business cannot be regarded simply as one pressure group or interest group along with others, such as trade unions, environmental groups, welfare lobbyists, and so on. They constitute a power that in many cases is equal to that of government. And although their interests may well coincide with the interests of society at large – 'what is good for General Motors is good for the country' – this is not necessarily so. At the very least, what governments believe to be in the public interest is itself refracted through the lens of the particular interests of business. As Lindblom concludes, what we call democracy is in fact a compromise between the power of the vote and the power of business, with government negotiating the interface between the two.

Now it may be said that we have become so used to this situation that we take it for granted, even though it is at variance with received democratic ideas of political equality, the primacy of the representative process, and the responsiveness of government to a plurality of social interests and views. And if everything had stayed the same, there might be little ground for seeing it as a factor in the increasing level of dissatisfaction with government. Yet there are good reasons for believing that the sway of business interests over government has significantly increased since Lindblom's time, and that the balance between the respective powers of the vote and business has shifted in favour of the latter. I shall suggest a number of reasons for this.

the cost of elections

The enormously increased cost of election campaigns has made candidates and parties of all persuasions ever more reliant on contributions from wealthy individuals and businesses. This not only gives the latter a special influence over party policy which ordinary voters do not enjoy, but it also creates a tacit understanding over the granting of political favours to particular contributors, even thought there may be no explicit agreement to do so.

The dominance of 'special interests' over government and the legislative process has been taken furthest in the USA, where election costs are enormous. In 1996, a seat in the Senate cost the average victor between $4 and $5 million, and the presidential contest required tens of millions. By now these figures will have been inflated much further. In 2004, President Bush started his re-election campaign with a 'war chest' of $140 million. It is hardly surprising that large contributors, who may fund Republicans and Democrats alike, expect to see their donations rewarded through the promotion of legislation favourable to themselves, or the blocking of proposals which might damage their interests.

So it happens that proposals which enjoy a wide measure of popular support, such as universal health care, environmental protection or gun control get blocked in Congress. The drugs and health insurance companies mobilise their congressional supporters to block the first, the oil and automobile companies the second, and the gun manufacturers the third. At the same time, attempts to limit government subsidies and tax breaks to individual industries almost invariably fail. As a former Nobel prizewinner in economics put it, 'corporate welfare' always wins out over 'social welfare' when budgets get tight.

The 1990s saw determined pressure on government by US businesses to deregulate major sectors of the economy, such as energy, telecommunications and banking, and to prevent regulation where it was already lax. The accounting industry, for example, provided campaign contributions to over half the representatives in the House and over ninety per cent of senators between 1998 and 2000, to help head off moves to tighten accountancy rules. The resulting freedom from regulation, combined with a shift towards rewarding company directors and executives with share options, meant that company executives, their accountants and banks all had an incentive to collude in practices which grossly inflated the share prices of their companies. But it was their employees and the investing public who lost out when some of these companies went bust in the economic downturn. The most spectacular collapse was that of Enron, the world's biggest energy trading company, whose executives between them made over $1 billion from the timely sale of their shares, leaving employees with their pension funds destroyed. When, in response to public outcry, a number of congressional committees were set up to investigate the scandal, it turned out that as many as 212 of their 248 members had received campaign contributions either from Enron or its discredited accountants, Arthur Andersen.

Such distortions of the democratic process are not as extreme in the old democracies of Europe, but they have been moving in the same direction. France, Germany and Italy have all had serious scandals involving contributions to political parties in return for favours to business, and many believe that these simply represent the tip of an iceberg. In Britain, New Labour set out determinedly to woo business support before the 1997 election, and to reduce its financial dependency on the trade unions. It has seen its share of scandals as a result, including the Ecclestone affair (postponing the tobacco ban in motor racing), the Hinduja affair (accelerating applications for British passports) and the Draper affair (cash for access to the inside track to ministers). Less noticeable, because now routine, has been the practice of rewarding individual business supporters with seats in the upper chamber of Parliament (House of Lords), and positions on key government advisory bodies.

privatisation

One element in the increasing dependency of democratic politics on business, then, lies in the latter's contributions in cash and kind to improve the chances of candidates and parties in increasingly expensive electoral contests. A second comes through the increasing dependency of government on the private sector for the delivery of basic public services. The UK has already seen the privatisation of utilities such as water, energy, telecommunications and public transport. Under the Labour Government's so-called 'private finance initiative', this process has been extended to the financing of key public building projects and their maintenance, and the running of some hospitals, schools and prisons, as well as most local services.

While claims for the economic advantage of such schemes have proved to be considerably inflated, they have brought with them significant disadvantages for the quality of democratic politics. There has been a loss of public accountability, as contractual terms have been kept secret for reasons of commercial confidentiality. There is the continuing danger that the public interest will be neglected or distorted to meet the needs of private profit, as has notably been the case in the recent history of British railway maintenance and safety. And as the railways have also shown, the government and the taxpayer is ultimately the guarantor of last resort, so that a service privatised supposedly to reduce public subsidy ends up with far more, because the government cannot afford for an essential service to be discontinued or disrupted. In negotiating and managing these arrangements, private providers have the whip hand of expertise that is no longer available in the public sector. So a policy which seemed at first sight to have the advantage of taking the provision of public services out of politics has produced an increasing dependency of government on business, and the reinforcement of close networks of relationship with it.

expert connections

Given the complexity of government in the contemporary world, governments have come to rely increasingly on advisory committees for guidance in the formulation and review of policy. As these have proliferated, so has their dominance by business people who have an interest in the policy area. More worrying has been the trend whereby the scientists who sit on such committees, and who are seemingly independent, often themselves have their research funded by private companies, whose interests they are consequently ready to promote.

In the previous chapter, I pointed to the important role that bodies such as universities can and should play in providing an alternative source of expertise as a check on government. As public funding of universities has declined relative to costs over the past decade and more, so universities throughout the Western world have increasingly had to rely on corporate financing of their research. Not only that, but the research committees which distribute public money for university research themselves have an eye to economic usefulness, and business people are well represented on them. In the UK, for example, the mission of the publicly funded research councils 'is to assist industry, commerce and government create wealth and improve the quality of life'. Similarly, with regard to the USA, one authoritative commentator has concluded that 'federal advisory committees that dispense funds now give private interests priority over public ones'.

The increased dependence of scientific research on business interests not only skews the direction of that research (e.g. into oil and gas, in preference to renewable energy). It also means that the technical advice received by government from academics is often much less independent than it appears. This trend has been exacerbated by governments appointing to advisory committees those experts who are more likely to tell them what they want to hear.

An issue which provided a watershed in public confidence in the independence of scientific advice in the UK was the BSE crisis. As a result of deregulation of the meat rendering industry by Mrs Thatcher's government, the practice became widespread of feeding to cattle sheep remains which had not been sterilised at the same temperatures as had previously been required. A resulting epidemic of brain disease in cattle (BSE) was hushed up by the agriculture department, and scientists investigating the possible transfer of the disease to other species were either denied access to data or had their work discredited. The department's own scientific advisory committee continued to downplay the risk to human health long after the disease had already skipped the species barrier, because of the damage this might cause to consumer confidence in the meat industry and to the profitable meat export trade. In the end, the damage to the industry was greater than if the disease had been dealt with effectively much earlier. Of longer-term consequence, however, has been a widespread loss of public confidence in the impartiality and integrity of science, especially in relation to the food industry and issues of public health.

A similar process can be seen in the USA, in relation to scientific research on climate change. Reminiscent of the way in which the tobacco industry previously poured huge sums into 'independent' research showing that the effects of smoking on health had been greatly exaggerated, so now the oil and energy industries are supporting science to challenge research about global warming and its effects. Such tendencies have chimed closely with the Bush government's resistance to environmental regulation. The Union of Concerned Scientists has expressed public concern about the way in which science is used by the administration. 'The administration has often manipulated the process through which science enters into its decisions,' they write. 'This has been done by placing people who have clear conflicts of interest in official posts or on scientific advisory committees ... by censoring or suppressing reports by the government's own scientists; and by simply not seeking independent scientific advice.' This process of what might be called the 'politicisation' of science inevitably reduces public confidence in its integrity, and in the government policies based upon it.

revolving doors

A final aspect of the way in which business and government have become virtually integrated is the 'revolving door' process, whereby business people are recruited directly into government, and retired politicians and civil servants move into corporate positions relevant to their previous departmental responsibilities. This is now an almost universal practice, but reached new heights with the Bush administration in the USA. Bush's own involvement in the Texas oil industry is well known. Vice President Cheney was Chief Executive Officer (CEO) of the oil service company Halliburton, which has won major contracts for reconstruction in Iraq. Secretary to the Treasury O'Neill served as president and CEO of the world's largest aluminium manufacturer, Alcoa. Secretary of Agriculture Veneman served on the board of the GM foods company Calgene. Secretary of Commerce Evans was chair and CEO of the oil and gas company Tom Brown Inc. Secretary of Energy Abraham, when senator for Michigan, received more in campaign contributions from the automobile industry than any other candidate. Secretary of Health Thompson, when formerly a governor, received large campaign contributions from tobacco firm Philip Morris. And so on.

nothing to worry about?

Now, in response to all this evidence about the close relationship between contemporary government and business interests, it is possible to make the argument I set out from Charles Lindblom at the start of this section. A robust market economy is necessary to the well-being of everyone. A key task of government is to pursue policies for the economy that will encourage business investment and growth. Who better to advise on such policies than the company executives on whose decisions that investment and growth depends?

If this were all, it would still be a matter of concern from a democratic point of view that one relatively small section of society, however important, were given a privileged position in the counsels of government. Yet we have seen that over the past decade or two it has gone much further than this. Policies in the public interest have become seriously distorted and in some cases blocked altogether in favour of the private interests of particular sectors of business. Individual companies have been able to buy privileged access to government through the contributions they make to the election expenses of candidates and parties. The privatisation of public utilities and services has introduced potentially significant conflicts of interest between company profits and the interests of service consumers, and has led to a loss of public accountability in the private contracts with government and in the operation of services. The independence and integrity of science that are necessary to confidence in government policy and its accountability have become compromised by the spread of business sponsorship of academic research, and by government politicisation of the interface between scientific expertise and policy making.

Such practices may go unnoticed by the general public for a long while, and only arouse concern among a narrow class of political observers and specialists. Yet it only takes a major scandal – and there have been a number of these in all countries – to bring to the surface a more widespread if vague sense of disquiet that government is not being run in the people's interests. The democratic ideas of popular control and political equality that I outlined in the previous two chapters, and the institutional means for their realisation, do not seem to be functioning in practice as they should. The supremacy of the electoral process in determining the direction of government policy, transparency in the use of taxpayers' money and the even-handedness of government in relation to social interests and views all seem to have become significantly compromised. This process may have gone much further in some countries than others, where the democratic aspects of political life are more carefully protected. Nevertheless, the process has been evident everywhere, and it forms part of the explanation for a decline in public confidence in representative institutions.

Why has this process been common to so many countries at the same time? The end of the 1980s saw the convergence of two significant shifts in the politico-economic conditions of all Western countries. One was the acceptance among economic thinkers and policy makers of a pure version of free-market ideas: market good; state bad. This had fuelled the drive to privatise public utilities and services during the 1980s, and to deregulate business activities. Rather than separating economic activity from politics, however, this change simply made government even more dependent on business, as we have seen. The second change was the collapse of the socialised economic systems of the Communist world. By providing a pole of opposition to capitalism, and the possibility of an alternative to it, these had at least exercised some moderating influence upon it from without. Their disintegration intensified what Joseph Stiglitz has called the 'irrational exuberance' of the 'Roaring Nineties', in which the unrestrained pursuit of private economic interests became the supreme virtue for public life.

A third change in economic conditions, which is linked to the other two, has had an even more profound effect upon the activity of government and the prospects for democracy. This is the process known as economic 'globalisation', which has called into question the capacity of any government to determine on its own the policy agenda for its country. This will form the subject of the next section.

decline in government capacity

As we saw in chapter 1, the system of representative democracy was developed as a means for realising democratic ideas at the level of the nation state. Democratic governments have been seen as being representative of and accountable to a given *people* inhabiting a clearly defined territory. A basic assumption of democratic politics has been that governments have been able to make policy for their country without external interference or constraint. Even where governments have deferred to domestic business, they have at least been able to set the broad terms of economic and social policy for the country as a whole. Whatever flaws or limitations such policies might have had, at least they were domestically determined by conditions within the country.

This domestic control by governments over their policy agenda has now been called into question by the process known as economic 'globalisation'. 'Globalisation' is a vogue word, whose precise meaning and significance are hotly debated. Yet it does point to real economic processes at work at the international level, which substantially limit the policies national governments can pursue.

Take trade and investment, for example. The last two decades have seen an enormous increase in international trade and investment, and in the growth of multinational companies which have the capacity to switch their production and investment between countries, according to where the conditions are most favourable. 'Most favourable' means not only where wages are low, but where corporation taxes are light, company contributions to social security are minimal, and regulations over working and environmental conditions are lax. This freedom of movement by multinationals tends to penalise governments which seek to maintain standards of social welfare, environmental regulation or tax regimes that are significantly out of line with their competitors. In addition, many of the measures which governments have used in the past to develop a coherent industrial policy for their country are no longer possible under international trade rules.

Equally significant has been the liberalisation of financial markets and the enormous growth in speculative funds, which can be switched between financial products and national currencies at breathtaking speed. The power of financial markets limits the control that governments have over their national economies in two ways: it discourages them from pursuing any policies, such as deficit budgeting, or high welfare spending, that are considered questionable by orthodox financial opinion; it also creates much greater unpredictability for governments, as they can never be sure that their currencies will not be subject to sudden speculative attack, as happened for example in the East Asian crisis of 1997. Almost overnight, international opinion changed from talking up the countries in the region as engines of growth, to regarding them as economic basket cases. 'Overall', one commentator concludes, 'these changes substantially reduce the effectiveness and reliability of national economic policy instruments ... the power of governments has diminished substantially relative to private markets and firms.'

What has this to do with democracy? Democracy is about the people of a country exercising significant control over government through elections and other political processes. Yet that control is worth little if the government itself is not in control of the policies that matter for the well-being of its citizens, but has lost it to external actors and economic forces beyond its reach. One very noticeable consequence of these external constraints is that the difference between the programmes of the political parties is substantially reduced, as parties of the Left abandon traditional social-democratic programmes of economic intervention, high welfare spending and employment regulation, and become virtually indistinguishable from parties of the centre-Right in their economic policies. This has happened in most countries, and has been particularly evident in the case of New Labour in Britain. It is hardly surprising that, without meaningful choice, electoral and party democracy tends to atrophy.

intensified inequalities

Economic globalisation has one further consequence that affects the quality of democracy. At root, globalisation is about the freeing up and expansion of markets, to encourage economic activity and growth to the general benefit. But markets also intensify inequalities between people, by rewarding those already advantaged in terms of personal and financial resources, and penalising the disadvantaged. The last twenty years or so have seen a corresponding intensification of economic inequality both within countries and between them. Table 3.2 demonstrates this effect in the developed 'Anglo-Saxon' economies, where the deregulation of markets has been most marked. Table 3.3 shows the increasing divergence in the Gross Domestic Product (GDP) between the high income and low income countries.

Within the developed economies, this pattern of inequality has produced a disadvantaged minority whose income and circum-stances have effectively excluded them from the quality of life that the rest of us have come to take for granted. And with this social exclusion comes political exclusion also, as people lose the capacity or will for any exercise of democratic citizenship. Within the developing economies, the intensification of inequality between countries has considerably increased the incentives for people to try

Table 3.2   Richer faster – growing inequality in the United Kingdom, United States, Australia and New Zealand

United Kingdom: Percentage share of household income

	1979	2001
Top 20 per cent.	37	45
Bottom 20 per cent.	9	6

Source: House of Commons *Written Answer* 27 Oct 2003 : Column 41W.

United States: Percentage share of household income

	1979	2001
Top 20 per cent.	44	50
Bottom 20 per cent.	4	4

Source: US Census Bureau 2002 'Historical Income Tables – Income Equality' *Current Population Survey, Annual Demographic Supplements*, http://www.census.gov. Accessed April 2004.

Australia: Percentage share of household income

	1975/6	1993/4
Top 20 per cent.	39.7	44.5
Bottom 20 per cent.	5.6	4.2

Source: Australian Bureau of Statistics (various years) *Household Expenditure Surveys*.

New Zealand: Percentage share of gross personal income

	1982	1996
Top 20 per cent.	48	51
Bottom 20 per cent.	5	5

Source: Statistics New Zealand 1999 *New Zealand Now – Incomes (Census 1996)* Reference Reports.

to migrate to the developed ones, where even the conditions of the most disadvantaged appear infinitely preferable to their own.

Now immigration is a hugely contentious subject, but one that cannot be avoided in any discussion of contemporary democracy. It

Table 3.3   Inequality between the global North and South. Average
GDP per capita (US$)

	1970	1980	1990	2000
High Income Countries[1]	2,733	11,483	22,050	27,591
Low Income Countries[2]	142	370	270	211

Source: Global Policy Forum 2004 'Average GDP per Capita In 20 High Income
Countries And 20 Low Income Countries, 1970–2000', citing IMF *World Economic
Outlook*, http://www.globalpolicy.org. Accessed April 2004.
1. High Income Countries. Australia, Austria, Belgium, Canada, China P.R., Hong Kong,
Denmark, Finland, France, Germany, Iceland, Ireland, Japan, Luxembourg, Netherlands,
Norway, Singapore, Sweden, Switzerland, United Kingdom and United States.
2. Low Income Countries. Burkina Faso, Burundi, Central African Rep., Chad, Ethiopia,
Ghana, Guinea-Bissau, Kenya, Madagascar, Malawi, Mali, Mozambique, Myanmar,
Nepal, Niger, Nigeria, Rwanda, Sierra Leone, Tanzania and Uganda.

is not just that it has become a major political issue in all developed
countries; it has become so partly because the presence of migrants
with a different culture and way of life challenges people's sense of
who they are as a nation, and who properly belongs to it as an equal
citizen. While many among the host population will welcome the
presence of immigrants as a source of cultural and economic diversity, many will also see it as changing the character of neighbourhood and country without their having been consulted. And of these
latter, many are to be found among the most disadvantaged sections
of the host society, and living in neighbourhoods where immigrants
tend to be concentrated.

It would not be far-fetched to see the inequalities generated by
economic globalisation, which produce simultaneously deprived
minorities in the developed countries and intensified pressures for
migration in developing ones, as lying at the root of the recent rise of
far-right political parties in most countries of Western Europe.
Parties with names such as the British National Party, the French
National Front etc. indicate their appeal to an archetypal idea of 'the
nation'. Their policies of zero immigration and the repatriation of
illegal immigrants and 'bogus' asylum seekers have achieved considerable popular resonance and electoral impact, and have tapped into
wider popular dissatisfaction with the governmental performance of
the mainstream parties. Immigrants have thus been made the all too
visible scapegoats for economic processes which governments have

proved relatively powerless to control, and the success of these parties has become symptomatic of a deeper democratic malaise.

regaining control?

Is it possible for governments to reassert any control over these forces of economic globalisation? The only way for them to do so is through co-operation in international organisations and treaty bodies, through which it might be possible to bring some measure of regulation to international business and finance, and some more positive harmonisation between different countries' economic policies. In fact, many of the problems now facing governments can only be addressed at the international level. This is most obviously true of environmental problems, such as global warming, resource depletion, pollution of the atmosphere and seas, and so on. But it applies equally to many aspects of economic and social life, where what happens in one country is affected by what happens outside it.

From this perspective, the European Union can be seen as an ambitious project by member governments to pool their sovereignty so that they can together achieve a measure of control over their economic environment which they cannot achieve on their own. So the development of a free market across Europe is counterbalanced by protection for minimum labour standards, trade union rights, environmental standards and social regulation. This common process of regulation is now so extensive that around seventy per cent of new legislation in the UK originates in Brussels, where it is subject to the approval of a ministerial council drawn from all member countries.

This solution to the problems of declining governmental capacity and control, however, brings its own problems for democracy, in turn. First, it is extraordinarily difficult to subject international institutions such as the European Union to meaningful democratic control. We constantly hear talk of the 'democratic deficit' in the EU, by which is meant that it obstinately remains an institution of political élites and policy experts, which is neither accountable nor responsive to the people. But then, secondly, who are 'the people' here? There is simply no common language, no common media of communication and no sense of common identity across the different European countries. Our identities have all been shaped at the national level, as British, French, Italian, Spanish etc., yet a considerable gap has opened up between this level at which we are used to conducting our democratic politics, and the level where many of the decisions affecting our lives are now taken. As I have shown, representative democracy was developed within and for the territory of the nation state. Yet that territorial level is now in the process of being relegated to a second plane, and it is not clear how democracy can be reconstructed at a higher European, let alone a global, level.

Different kinds of proposal for democratising international institutions will be considered at some length in chapter 5. For the moment, however, I shall simply summarise the argument of this section. We are trying to identify possible sources of disaffection among Western publics with their government and representative institutions. One source of disaffection is that the processes of economic globalisation have meant governments losing a measure of control and discretion over their economic and social policies; this loss of discretion has led to a decline in the difference between the major political parties, as they have all tried to adjust to the 'realities' of the international marketplace; and one form the resentment at this loss of control takes is support for parties of the extreme Right, whose scapegoating of immigrants attacks a symptom rather than the causes of the problem. At the same time, attempts to address the loss of control through the development of international institutions creates a new democratic deficit in its turn, by making government more remote from citizens, and less subject to democratic control and accountability.

US readers who have got this far may feel that nothing I have written in this section applies to their country. It is simply too large and too economically powerful to be subject to the same constraints as lesser nations. Indeed, it has played a large role in promoting the processes of economic globalisation which I have described. Nevertheless, it is not immune from their effects. The USA has lost manufacturing jobs at a steady rate to other countries; its huge trade deficit with the rest of the world is a potential source of instability for itself as well as others; its currency is no longer immune from international speculation, nor its territory from the effects of global warming or the pressures of migration. Attempts under President Bush to reassert control over some of these forces through protectionist measures have brought it into sharp conflict with the rest of the world, especially the European Union. And its 'go it alone' policies towards international treaties and institutions have caused considerable resentment among countries whose co-operation it will need in the future. As a huge power, it naturally has more control and discretion over policy than others, but it cannot isolate itself from the processes to which all are now subject.

declining credibility

Politicians have rarely inspired great trust. They usually come at the bottom in opinion polls asking voters which social and political institutions they have confidence in. Reasons for this are to be found in the nature of politics as an activity. It is based upon persuasion, on presenting a policy or course of action in the best possible light, so as to maximise support for it. It involves cutting deals and making compromises, sometimes quite shabby ones, in order to attain something more worthwhile. In politics, therefore, there is constantly a gap between what politicians are doing or achieving, and what they say they are doing or achieving – a gap between their public justifications for a policy and their actual reasons for pursuing it. Successful politicians are skilful at obscuring these gaps, but they are always vulnerable to their becoming exposed. And when they are, public confidence and trust are eroded. This is nothing new. 'Get thee glass eyes', wrote Shakespeare, 'And, like a scurvy politician, seem / To see things thou dost not.'

the politics of spin

What appears to have qualitatively changed over the past fifteen years or so can be summed up by the word 'spin'. If by 'spin' we simply mean a concern with public image and good public relations, then this has always been part of the politician's stock-in-trade. Relatively new are the huge budgets now assigned to government communication and its staffing, the ruthlessness and degree of political co-ordination employed to ensure that everyone is 'on message', and the preoccupation with news management and presentation. As governments' scope for achieving their goals has shrunk, so their preoccupation with presentation has grown proportionately. Appearance has become the new reality; even the news story is often not about a programme or policy but about how it is 'spun'. We no longer raise our eyebrows when governments create diversions so as to 'bury bad news', when they 'dig for dirt' on their critics or opponents rather than address their arguments, or when they marginalise critical experts and induce others to give opinions favourable to government policy. Yet our confidence in their integrity is reduced as a consequence.

Now many politicians argue that the blame for this situation lies with the media: with radio, television and the press, which are the main means through which they communicate with the public. They point out, with some justification, that there has been a systematic 'dumbing down' in the media presentation of politics, a confusion of news and opinion, a concentration on personalities and their foibles rather than on policies, and the fostering of a climate of cynicism about politicians in general. As a consequence, politicians in government have to work especially hard to get their message across, and to do so twenty-four hours a day in the new context of rolling news programmes.

Of course, the simplest way of doing this is for politicians to control media outlets directly: through ownership of private media by themselves, their parties or their supporters, or through government control of public broadcasting. A basic condition of a democratic society, however, is that there should be a plurality of privately owned media channels, and fair access to public service broadcasting for opposition politicians and voices critical of government. In many new and restored democracies, this condition is not met. Even in some of the 'old' democracies, it is under threat, most notably in Italy, where Prime Minister Berlusconi combines his far-reaching ownership of private television with tight government control over the publicly owned media. In countries where the condition is met, however, and there is a genuine plurality of media channels, governments have to work much harder to get their message across, and the arts of spin have become particularly well developed.

spinning to excess

The Labour government, which came into office in the UK in 1997, carried the practice of spin to unprecedented heights, and its methods and record are worth examining for that reason, as an extreme example of a more general phenomenon. The party had been deeply scarred during seventeen years of opposition by a consistently hostile press, and by the latter's treatment of any internal party disagreements as evidence of chronic division or personalised power struggles. Tony Blair came into office determined to control the news agenda, to co-ordinate communication across government, and to marginalise anyone in government or party who was not 'on message'. He broke precedent by appointing his own press secretary, Alastair Campbell, a former journalist and party supporter, as director of communications in Downing Street, with authority to instruct civil servants and to appoint special advisors from the media to communications posts in the individual ministries.

The ruthlessness with which Campbell sought to control the news and 'fight for every headline' became legendary, and the methods were not always pretty: bullying journalists, pressurising civil servants, briefing against ministers who were out of favour, pre-empting Parliament by leaking government initiatives in advance, giving privileged access to information to selected newspapers and journalists in return for favourable coverage, and so on. And his appointees and followers in the individual ministries proved equally obsessive, 'perpetually promoting the next story or trying to recycle what had already been announced'.

All this might have mattered less if it had been necessary to achieve an ambitious programme for government or even a set of clear political principles. But Labour had entered office with a timid agenda, and no clear principles or ideology, other than a rather vacuous 'third way'. The contrast between Labour's lack of ambition and its huge Parliamentary majority was especially stark. And after some years it began to seem as if the control and presentation of information had become an end in itself. Where the Tory Party had become discredited in government for 'sleaze' (a climate of petty corruption), New Labour was now discredited for 'spin-doctoring' and 'control freakery'. Towards the end of Labour's first term in office, Philip Gould, Blair's chief focus-group guru, was complaining that 'the New Labour brand has been badly contaminated ... It has been undermined by a combination of spin, lack of conviction and apparently lack of integrity'. And even Blair himself seemed to recognise that 'some of the questionable routines that had been put in place to control the flow of information and to grab the headlines had developed a momentum of their own and were no longer capable of being restrained'.

The excesses of New Labour management of the news were not fully exposed, however, until its second term of office, from 2001. Two episodes proved defining moments of the era. The first was when the political advisor in the transport ministry, Jo Moore, circulated an e-mail on 11 September 2001 saying that this was 'a good day to bury bad news', of which there was plenty in the railway industry. The subsequent leaking of this e-mail caused a political storm. The failure of the minister, Stephen Byers, to dismiss rather than reprimand her created a running sore, from which further revelations continued to seep: that she had instructed civil servants to give personal briefings against Bob Kiley, the London Transport Commissioner, with whom the department was in disagreement, and that she was involved in a purported attempt to publish accident statistics on the day of Princess Margaret's funeral. In the end, she was forced to resign, along with the department's head of communications, and Stephen Byers followed soon after.

This episode was marked by repeated friction between the press and Downing Street communications officials, whose attempts to control the damage only made it worse. Yet this friction was eclipsed by the full frontal assault on the BBC by Campbell himself in early summer 2003, in what became known as the Gilligan affair. The BBC reporter had suggested in an early morning broadcast that intelligence sources had expressed disquiet about a government dossier on Saddam's weapons of mass destruction, in which intelligence had been 'sexed up' at Downing Street's request. Campbell's obsessive pursuit of this story, and the BBC's refusal to apologise for it, led to enormous pressure on Gilligan's source, Dr Kelly, and to his suicide. When the subsequent Hutton enquiry cleared Downing Street of all wrongdoing and laid all the blame on the BBC, there was widespread disbelief, as this contradicted evidence of repeated pressure on the intelligence services that the enquiry had itself exposed. Given their respective track records, the public proved to have much more confidence in the credibility of the BBC than in Downing Street or Campbell himself, whose retirement had been announced early on in the course of the enquiry.

What gave this latter episode such dramatic force, of course, was that it involved an issue of peace and war, in which there was already widespread public disquiet about the government's justification for going to war against Iraq. In the UK, the prospect of the war had divided the country from the outset, and the government had its work cut out to convince the public of its merits. In retrospect, these efforts seem to have betrayed a lack of sincerity, in that war had already been decided upon in advance, and the UN resolutions and the arms inspection process were merely designed to legitimate it rather than prevent it. This impression was reinforced by the leaks that subsequently emerged from within government: about the political manipulation of intelligence; about the bugging of UN delegations; about the prevarications in the Attorney General's opinion about the legality of the war, and so on.

In the USA, it took longer for the disquiet about the Iraq war to surface, as the post 9/11 climate of insecurity had made the concept of 'pre-emptive defence' much more readily acceptable. But by the middle of 2004 most of the claims underpinning President Bush's justification for the war had been shown to be bogus. No weapons of mass destruction could be found in Iraq, despite exhaustive searches. The suggested links between Saddam and the perpetrators of the 9/11 outrage were shown to be groundless. Iraq had become a new focus for terrorism and a new source of grievance in the Middle East, which made Western lives more, not less, vulnerable. And the concocted images of Iraqi rejoicing at their 'liberation' had been overtaken by the chaos brought by the coalition's failure to plan for the peace, and by the images of torture from Abu Ghraib. The exposure of the gulf between government claims and the actual reality started to undermine confidence in the President's own competence and credibility.

declining confidence

While it is too soon to assess the long-term effects of the Iraq war on public confidence in government, it will have done nothing to stem its decline. Yet does the integrity of government matter that much? Can democracy not live perfectly easily with dishonesty, provided it is not corruption for personal gain? Doesn't the activity of politics, as I have already suggested, require its practitioners to be 'economical with the truth'?

There are a number of answers that can be given to these objections. None of us likes being taken for a ride, or being made a fool of. A number of the spin-doctoring practices revealed in the UK under New Labour have been demeaning, and because they were done in our name and with our money, they have demeaned us also. More importantly, government depends at a number of levels on people's co-operation; if we no longer believe what politicians tell us, we will fail to support them when it really matters. This is why 'spin' is ultimately self-defeating. The best demonstration of that lies in the history of countries under Communist rule, where the government enjoyed a monopoly of public means of communication, but after a while few people believed a word they were told. As a result, their support could not be mobilised, even for much-needed economic reforms.

Perhaps most serious of all, the decline of trust in politicians has come to undermine confidence in wider groups of people, whose independence is important to the effectiveness and accountability of government. As the story of this chapter shows, there has been a steady process of politicisation of a number of key groups whose credibility depends upon their independence: the intelligence services, government legal advisors, scientific experts on government advisory committees, the civil service itself. This has happened when governments have appealed to their independence to bolster public support for a policy, only for it to emerge that the experts had been 'leant on' to come up with the answers the government wanted to hear. Again, once that image of independence is lost, it is difficult for it to be recaptured, and a key instrument in the credibility and accountability of government policy is weakened as a consequence. Democracy is not just about electing a government and then letting it do what it likes. Government has to be exposed to continuing scrutiny and accountability by bodies the public can have confidence in.

conclusion

Readers may feel that in this chapter I have presented an excessively gloomy account of the democratic condition in the 'old' democracies. One of the distinctive features of democratic systems, however, is their capacity for self-renewal, and the way in which forces that erode democracy are open to challenge and correction. So it is important by way of conclusion to suggest some possible strategies for reform, not so much by way of a blueprint, but to indicate the kind of direction that a process of democratic renewal might take. In the absence of such a prospect, disaffection tends to degenerate into mere apathy.

It should be evident from what I have written that much of its story is one of politicians reacting to conditions that have escaped their control, whether it be the deregulation of the economy, the globalisation of markets, or the emergence of twenty-four hours' news media and the personalisation of political reporting. Yet they are not powerless when it comes to restoring a measure of integrity to democratic government, as efforts already in process in some countries have shown. While much depends upon the particular circumstances of each country, the broad direction of a process of renewal is suggested by the following:

* reducing the power of money over politics through tight limits on election expenditure for candidates and parties, the annual publication of audited party accounts and sources of income, and a compulsory 'register of interests' for all elected representatives;

- reducing the sway of special interests over government by rules requiring the transparency and inclusiveness of government consultative procedures, and by prohibiting elected representatives from taking part in debates and decisions on issues affecting organisations from which they have accepted money or in which they have a financial interest;
- limiting concentrations of media ownership, and guaranteeing the independence from government and the impartiality and inclusiveness of all publicly owned and subsidised media;
- reversing the politicisation of agencies, the independence of whose advice is important for the credibility of government policy, e.g. through independent appointment procedures, transparent codes of conduct, declarations of interest where appropriate, and so on;
- ensuring an effective freedom of information regime and a public interest defence for 'whistleblowers'.

These measures do not touch the issues of globalisation and the international aspects of democracy, which will be considered in chapters 4 and 5. Nor do they include more radical and innovative forms of democratic renewal, which will be explored in chapter 6. Even so, some would see them as hopelessly idealistic, since they have to be implemented by the very politicians who are locked into current patterns of working, and have an interest in perpetuating them. Yet the effects of popular pressure should not be discounted, since it has already brought about reforms in a number of countries. In the UK, for example, public indignation at 'sleaze' under the Tory government contributed to the establishment of an independent commissioner for parliamentary standards, and the development of codes of conduct for MPs and government officials.

Some would argue that what is really needed is a cultural shift towards a more honest relationship between politicians and the public: one in which our leaders treat us as adults, acknowledge the dilemmas they face and the constraints within which they have to operate, and admit their fallibility. And we for our part should reduce our expectations of what they can achieve. Politics, in other words, should become mundane and matter of fact. In the process, however, we might lose what we also look to politicians to provide – a sense of hope and excitement, and visions of a better world. Without reaching for the impossible, even that which is possible may not be attained. I personally see no reason why a democracy should not allow us to hope for the best, while also having effective mechanisms in place to protect us from the worst.

further reading

Hutton, Will. *The World We're In*. London: Abacus, 2003 (US title, *Declaration of Interdependence*. Boston: Little, Brown).

Jones, Nicholas. *The Control Freaks*. London: Politicos, 2002.

Lindblom, Charles. *Politics and Markets*. New York: Basic Books, 1977.

Monbiot, George. *The Captive State*. London: Pan Macmillan, 2001.

Moore, Michael. *Dude, Where's My Country?* London and New York: Penguin Books, 2003.

Palast, Greg. *The Best Democracy Money Can Buy*. London: Pluto Press, 2002.

Pharr, Susan and Robert Putnam, eds. *Disaffected Democracies*. Princeton: Princeton University Press, 2000.

Pitcher, George. *The Death of Spin*. London: John Wiley and Sons, 2003.

Rampton, Sheldon and John Stauber. *Weapons of Mass Deception*. London: Constable and Robinson; New York: Penguin, 2003.

Stiglitz, Joseph. *The Roaring Nineties: Seeds of Destruction*. London and New York: Penguin Books, 2003.

success and setback in the new and emergent democracies

The term 'new and emergent democracies' refers to those countries which have made a transition from different forms of authoritarian rule to competitive electoral democracy in the period since 1980. With the exception of the former Communist countries, these all come from the developing regions of the South – Africa, Asia and Latin America. Some of these have had democratic systems of government before, sometimes alternating with periods of authoritarian rule: the preferred UN designation is 'new and restored democracies' to indicate this. I propose to use these different terms interchangeably, since it will be clear what they refer to. Although each of these countries has its own unique history and distinctive trajectory from authoritarian government, together they can be seen as part of a common 'wave' of democratisation that began in the early 1980s and developed increasing momentum during the early 1990s.

Before searching for explanations of this new democratic 'wave', it will be worth getting a clearer sense of its character. Table 4.1 gives figures from the assessment by the US-based organisation *Freedom House* of the number of countries which have become 'free' in their terms since their first global survey in 1972. Although there is no universal agreement about the validity of the methods whereby the organisation reaches its conclusions, they nevertheless give a

Table 4.1   Freedom House assessments of freedom and democracy

Number of countries in each category by region, 1972 and 2002						
	Free		Partly free		Unfree	
	1972	2002	1972	2002	1972	2002
World	43	89	38	56	69	47
Americas	13	23	9	10	4	2
W. Europe	18	24	4	1	3	0
Asia/Pacific	8	18	13	10	11	11
Cent. E. Europe, ex-USSR	0	12	0	9	9	6
Sub-Saharan Africa	2	11	9	22	28	15
Mid-East, N. Africa	2	1	3	4	14	13

Source: Freedom House 2003, http://www.freedomhouse.org. Accessed April 2004.

rough-and-ready snapshot of the changes that have taken place over this period. A fully 'free' or 'democratic' country in *Freedom House* terms is one which combines political rights (to form political parties and contest elections under universal suffrage, in which there is significant choice between candidates for government office) with civil liberties (personal freedoms, freedoms of the press, belief, association and minority rights). This list conforms roughly to the first two components of democracy I set out in chapter 2. Countries whose citizens enjoy none of these rights are classified as 'unfree', and those where only some are enjoyed are 'partly free'. Table 4.1 sets out changes in the different regions of the world between 1972 and 2002, a period which has also seen an increase in the number of countries becoming independent, and so counting in the figures for 2002.

Two points are worth noting about this table. The first concerns the regional distribution of the changes. The Americas, Asia/Pacific, the former USSR and its satellite countries, and sub-Saharan Africa, are the regions where democratisation has been taking place. We should, however, be aware of the few countries from these regions that have remained free and democratic throughout this period: India and Japan in Asia, Botswana in sub-Saharan Africa, Jamaica and other former British colonies in the West Indies. The countries of Western Europe were already mostly free and democratic in 1972, with the exception of Greece, Portugal and Spain under authoritarian regimes of different kinds. North Africa and the Middle East, on the other hand, is a region that has not been significantly affected by the recent wave of democratisation, for reasons that will be explored later.

A second point concerns what lies behind the category of the 'partly free'. In most cases, these are countries which have introduced democratic elections, often ones that have been declared free and fair by international observers. Yet they enjoy no stable rule of law, no guarantee of basic citizen rights, and government may be marked by widespread corruption. We should not assume, therefore, that a country is 'democratic' just because it has introduced competitive elections for public office. Elections, while important, do not comprise the whole of democracy. On this basis, the authors of the *Freedom House* survey have concluded that, although the number of electoral democracies in the world increased from 66 in 1987 to 121 in 2002, only 89 of these counted as fully free or democratic.

Competitive elections for public office by universal suffrage, then, comprise a necessary but not a sufficient condition for full democracy. Yet their achievement marks a decisive break with a previous authoritarian regime, and an important staging post in the process of institutionalising the democratic practices I outlined in chapter 2. So, a different way of charting the wave of democracy over the past twenty-five years is to look at the dates when different countries instituted (or re-instituted) competitive elections, mostly with a new constitution or constitutional revision to accompany them. These are set out in table 4.2.

The list is not exhaustive, but it gives a fair idea of the respective timing and regional spread of these transitions from authoritarian rule. The 1980s saw an end to military regimes or military-backed governments in much of Latin America and South-East and East Asia, often through a gradual process, though marked by dramatic episodes of popular struggle. The early 1990s, on the other hand, saw much more rapid transitions to electoral democracy in sub-Saharan Africa and the Communist countries of East and Central Europe, as single-party regimes gave way under different forms of popular pressure. The huge federal states of Indonesia and Nigeria were significant latecomers to this process of political change, only introducing competitive elections at the end of the 1990s.

How are we to explain this rapid and widespread success of electoral democracy across the world? Part of the explanation lies in the loss of legitimacy of previous authoritarian regimes, and the way each type in different manner had reached an impasse in its system

Table 4.2 Dates of transition to multi-party elections in selected countries, 1980–2000

1980	Bolivia
1984	Argentina, Uruguay
1985	Brazil
1987	Philippines, South Korea, Taiwan
1989	Chile
1990	Czech Republic, Hungary, Latvia, Namibia, Poland
1991	Bangladesh, Bulgaria, Gabon, Nepal, Russia
1992	Estonia, Ghana, Guinea, Kenya, Lithuania, Mongolia, Thailand
1993	Tanzania
1994	El Salvador, Malawi, Mozambique, South Africa
1999	Indonesia, Nigeria

Source: *The World Guide 2003/2004.*

of rule. The *military regimes* of Latin America and Asia gave way because the cost of excluding the population from the political process became too high, and continuing human rights abuses led to a decline in the political support they had once enjoyed. The *Communist governments* of Central/Eastern Europe collapsed once President Gorbachev made it clear that Moscow would no longer use force to maintain them, while in the USSR itself Gorbachev had concluded that necessary economic reforms were not possible without a relaxation of central political control. The *one-party systems* of sub-Saharan Africa decayed from within, as ageing rulers clung onto power in the face of increasingly adverse economic conditions and popular unrest. In South Africa and Namibia, *white minority rule* could no longer be sustained under the pressure of external economic sanctions and internal armed struggle.

Despite these divergent patterns of terminal decay in the different types of authoritarian regime, there was one factor common to them all. That was the attraction to their peoples of a democratic form of government, with its promise of political freedoms, protection for human rights and a government more responsive to popular demands. And the peoples themselves showed that they were prepared to struggle for it. All the transitions to democracy were marked by popular mobilisations, whether in the form of student protests, workers' strikes, women's campaigns for human rights, or the mass peaceful demonstrations of the 'velvet revolutions' in Eastern Europe in 1989. And the success of democratic struggle in one country served to embolden those in other countries, so that the idea of a democratic 'wave' gaining momentum as it moved forward did not seem far-fetched.

A further contributing factor was a change in the climate of international relations. During the Cold War with the Soviet Union, Western governments had been prepared to support military dictatorships and other authoritarian regimes in the developing world where they saw these as a bulwark against Communism. With the end of the Cold War in the late 1980s, Western priorities shifted to support for democratisation, and their development aid was increasingly made conditional upon a country's progress in democracy and human rights. How far this leverage helped bring change in individual countries is difficult to assess. Yet it contributed to an international environment which was conducive to democratisation and, equally important, it made it difficult for countries to revert back to authoritarian rule once free elections had been introduced.

Can we say, then, that democracy has now triumphed across the world? As an idea, or an ideal to strive for, perhaps it has. It is difficult to imagine the previous forms of authoritarian government, under life presidents or the permanent rule of a single party, achieving legitimacy or popular support again, though new military coups, such as in Pakistan in 1999, can never be ruled out. Opinion polls taken in countries that have recently democratised show consistent majorities of the population supporting democratic rule against authoritarian alternatives, though much smaller percentages express satisfaction with the way democracy is actually experienced in their own country. Figures for selected countries in sub-Saharan Africa and Latin America are shown in table 4.3.

When looking at such figures, it is important to keep in mind the distinction already made between the transition from authoritarian rule to what I call 'electoral democracy', and the much longer drawn-out process of realising and consolidating the fully democratic arrangements that I outlined in chapter 2. These include the effective guarantee of citizen rights through the rule of law, an elected government that remains fully accountable to the public, and civil society associations and media of communication that are independent of government and representative of different strands of public

Table 4.3   Support for democracy against alternatives, and satisfaction with it. Selected countries from Africa and Latin America, 2000

	Supporting democracy against alternatives[1] 2002	Very satisfied or satisfied with democracy in practice[2] 2002
Ghana	82	71
Malawi	71	47
Namibia	69	54
Nigeria	68	35
Kenya	80	79
South Africa	57	44
African average	64	54
Argentina	65	8
Brazil	37	17
Chile	59	50
Mexico	63	21
Peru	55	16
Venezuela	73	35
Latin America average	55	32

1. Percentage of respondents agreeing with the statement 'Democracy is preferable to any other kind of government'.
2. Percentage of respondents expressing the view that they are very or fairly satisfied 'with the way democracy works in (their country)'.

Source: Globalbarometer, http://www.globalbarometer.org. Accessed April 2004.

opinion. Although a reversion to authoritarian rule may be unlikely, therefore, many countries are finding it difficult to progress beyond a type of democracy which has all the trappings of electoral competition between parties but in which basic rights are insecure, government is unresponsive to people's needs, and significant sections of the population are alienated from the political process altogether.

We could therefore distinguish two phases in the process of democratisation: the first, a transition from authoritarian rule to electoral democracy, which can be accomplished quite rapidly; and a second, much longer drawn-out phase, whose precise end-point may be unclear. The first of these phases is marked by the very different legacies which the democratising countries carry with them from the previous authoritarian systems: from military rule, Communist government, other one-party systems, or white minority rule, respectively. In the second phase, of consolidating or deepening democracy, these differences of origin become less significant in the face of common difficulties which all these countries confront in realising a form of democracy that can satisfy the expectations of their peoples. A discussion of the challenges involved in these two distinct phases will form the subject of the remainder of this chapter.

legacies of transition

In this section, I shall consider the different legacies that democratic countries carry with them in their transition from different types of authoritarian regime. Each type produces a different set of problems which have to be resolved on the way to establishing a new form of political system with competitive elections and universal suffrage. I shall consider each of the four types already mentioned in turn.

military rule

Of all the problems that have to be confronted in the transition from military regimes to electoral democracy, two are particularly acute. The first is how to ensure sufficient support within the military for a new civilian regime so as to keep them from overthrowing the government again, when they manifestly have the physical power to do so. The second is how to satisfy the demands for justice from those who have suffered human rights violations at the hands of the military, and from their relatives. These requirements typically conflict with one another. Which matters more: the *political* need to keep the military 'on side' in the new democracy, or the requirements of *justice* for the dead and injured?

How these competing imperatives have been resolved in practice has depended on the manner in which military rule has ended:

whether through a rapid collapse of authority, or a gradual transition in which the military has been able to negotiate its terms with the successor civilian government. Argentina and Chile provide two contrasting examples from Latin America. In Argentina, the military junta was discredited by its defeat in the Malvinas or Falklands war of 1982, and could not protect its leaders from prosecution for their responsibility in the 'disappearance' of nearly ten thousand political opponents. Even so, the newly elected President Alfonsin had to put down four military uprisings between 1987 and 1989, and to agree a law of impunity for lesser military personnel who had been 'only obeying orders'. In Chile, by contrast, the terms of the settlement negotiated by General Pinochet for the return to civilian rule in 1989 included an impunity for human rights crimes from the outset, and a guarantee of continued military involvement in government, through reserved Cabinet posts and seats in the Senate, and his own continuation as Commander-in-Chief. The relatives of around three thousand 'disappeared' were able to learn the truth of what had happened to those killed under the regime through the work of a Truth and Reconciliation Commission, but not to obtain justice.

What happened to General Pinochet later, however, shows that such transition settlements may not last for ever. Pinochet was unexpectedly detained on charges of former human rights violations when on a visit to Britain in 1998. After his return to Chile, his immunity from prosecution was removed, though he was declared medically unfit actually to stand trial. The huge public demonstrations both for and against the general which these events provoked in Chile revealed a society still deeply divided in its assessment of the former military regime. At the international level, however, Pinochet's detention in Britain showed that domestic immunities from prosecution for the worst human rights violations would no longer be recognised abroad, a historic development that may act as a restraining influence on future dictators.

communist government

The transition to electoral democracy in the former Communist countries has consisted of multiple transitions simultaneously: the breakup of an empire and a radical shift of relations between states; the end of the command economy and the introduction of a free-market system; the collapse of the Communist party monopoly over state and society and the transition to electoral competition with free associational life. In no other countries has democratisation been associated with such simultaneous upheavals, or carried such a difficult legacy.

end of an empire

The collapse of Communism brought with it the end of the Soviet empire, and the creation of some fifteen independent states on the western border of Russia, in the Caucasus and in central Asia. Although all these states had been Soviet republics with their own administrations, in many of them the declarations of independence provoked secessionist movements, which have dogged them ever since. Even those without outright secessionist movements have had substantial minorities which have proved difficult to integrate into the new state, and have experienced periods of ethnic conflict. Achieving independent statehood tends to bring with it an upsurge of nationalist sentiment, to the disadvantage of those who do not fit into the majority definition of nationhood, but who had felt more protected within the previous political framework.

Similar processes have been at work in the countries of Eastern Central Europe, even though these were always formally independent and not part of the USSR. The end of Communism brought about the unification of Germany and the division of Czechoslovakia into two separate states. It also intensified tensions between minorities and majorities in a number of countries where these had been either suppressed or managed by the ruling Communist party. Most damaging of all has been the experience of the former Yugoslavia, where the declaration of independence by Croatia with its Serb minority in 1991 provoked a war with the Serbian dominated Yugoslav Republic, and set a pattern of ethnic cleansing that was later repeated in Bosnia–Herzegovina and then in Kosovo.

The collapse of Communism, then, brought with it a seismic shift in the balance of political forces both between states and within them, making issues of nationhood problematic, and leaving a difficult legacy for most of the new democracies. Nor should we overlook the effect of loss of empire on Russia itself. For all that it remains a vast country with huge natural resources, democratisation has been associated with a substantial loss of national prestige as its status as one of the two global superpowers has disintegrated.

market economy

The Communist economic system involved a command economy, with central planning of production, controlled prices and public ownership of enterprises. After 1989, decisions were taken across most of the former Communist bloc, with the guidance of Western economists, to move rapidly to a free-market economy. The rapidity of the change caused enormous dislocation. Exposure to international competition left many enterprises uneconomic and forced them to close. Established supply chains and trading links were disrupted. Privatisation of state assets was rushed through without the legal infrastructure necessary to guarantee security of property and contracts, and created a Mafia-style capitalism. The prevailing neo-liberal economic orthodoxy in the West held that removing the state from the economy was sufficient for the free market to flourish, ignoring the complex institutional and regulatory framework built up over generations that enabled the West's own free market to operate.

The consequences for ordinary people were catastrophic, especially in Russia and the countries of the former Soviet Union. They had expected Western-style democracy and markets to bring an improvement in economic conditions. In place of the queues and shortages of the command economy, however, they experienced a collapse of living standards. Savings were wiped out by inflation. Unemployment soared. And the state did not have the tax resources to fund a system of social security, which had previously been organised around the workplace. It could not even pay many of its own employees. Illnesses such as TB once more became common, infant mortality rates increased sharply and life expectancy decreased.

Although conditions were not as severe in many of the countries of Eastern/Central Europe as in Russia itself, the decline in living standards proved general. Figure 4.1 shows the sharp decline after 1990, compared with other regions. So democracy came with a very high price tag for ordinary people. By the end of the 1990s conditions had mostly stabilised, especially in the European countries that were having to align their legal and financial systems with those of Western Europe in order to qualify for membership of the European Union. Yet the overall legacy of the rush to market has been substantial deprivation, and a huge increase in inequality between the winners and losers in the new competitive conditions, especially in Russia itself.

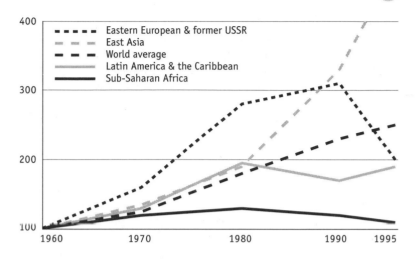

Figure 4.1.   *Growth in incomes in selected regions, 1960–1995*
Real per capita GDP (1960 = 100)
Source: World Bank data, 1997.

multiple parties

The change from any authoritarian system to electoral democracy requires the development of political parties to contest elections for governmental office. Under military dictatorships, where all parties are equally suppressed, the end of dictatorship often sees the re-emergence of previously established parties which have their historical bases of support among the different sections of the population. Under one-party systems, in contrast, a single party will have dominated public life maybe for decades, and will have become virtually inseparable from the state itself. Under Communist rule, the party also controlled most aspects of social life, so that there were no independent associations and no civic life as we know it.

As a consequence, when Communist rule came to an end, there were hardly any social movements or organisations, or even much social differentiation among the population, which might provide the basis for new political parties, or clear differences of principle or ideology between them. Large numbers of political parties were established, often simply as the personal following of individual leaders. Exceptions were the former Communist parties which, where they were not outlawed, transformed themselves into Western-type Social Democratic parties. And new parties embracing some variant of a nationalist platform enjoyed wide appeal, though these only intensified tendencies to minority exclusion already discussed. Although after a decade of electoral politics more settled party formations had taken shape in most of the former Communist countries, these still provide a rather uncertain basis for government formation or effective parliamentary scrutiny and accountability of the executive.

If we take these different dimensions of transition from Communist rule together – the rapid reconfiguration of states and nations, the dislocations of the move to a market economy and the weak social basis for stable political parties – it may seem surprising that democracy in any form could survive. In most of the countries of the former Soviet Union, it has only done so in a quite distorted and authoritarian form, with limited rule of law, government accountability or protection for citizen rights. In most of the countries of Eastern/Central Europe, by contrast, the process of candidacy for entry to the European Union has reinforced a more rapid and thorough democratisation, which by any standards must count as a remarkable achievement, given the difficult and multi-faceted nature of the transition that has been undertaken.

african single-party systems

Few one-party systems have achieved quite the same degree of control over society and state as under Communism. In the countries of East and Southern Africa, a form of one-party rule was established which emerged from the dominance of the parties that had won the first elections after independence in the 1960s. It was argued there that party competition and an institutionalised opposition to government were politically divisive and unsuited to an African tradition of more consensual forms of rule. The urgent tasks of economic development and nation building required everyone to pull together. People were able to air grievances through a variety of channels and party forums, and could choose between candidates for public office in competitive elections, provided they belonged to the one party that was legally recognised. This system was held to be just as democratic as 'multi-partyism'.

This argument had a certain plausibility in the early years of single-party rule, and Western donors even support a version of it today under President Museveni in Uganda. Yet there are serious drawbacks to a single-party system of representative democracy, which become more acute over time. First, it is difficult to mobilise support for alternative policy platforms without incurring the charge of splitting the party; so these alternatives tend not to get publicly debated as they do when they are taken up by a competing party. Secondly, political opponents to the party leadership can be consigned to the political wilderness by the simple expedient of expelling them from the party. Finally, and most seriously, it becomes exceedingly difficult to replace a party leader or president, even when they are long past their sell-by date, and popular dissatisfaction tends to be met by substantial repression.

Some of the drawbacks of the single-party system have persisted even after the return to party competition in the early 1990s. In some countries, such as Zambia and Malawi, the former presidents were decisively ejected from office in the first competitive elections. Yet the new political leaders inherited a tradition of overweening presidents and weak parliaments, and a pattern of stifling inconvenient public debate. And it has proved difficult to develop lasting party coalitions, either to sustain governments or to hold a coherent opposition together. In Kenya, President Moi was able to hold onto power for ten years after multi-party elections, through a combination of dividing, co-opting and suppressing different elements of the opposition. Some pessimistic commentators have concluded that the adoption of multi-party elections has been largely a device to satisfy Western donors, while the pattern of government and its relationship to the people has remained largely unaltered. At the least, it will take a long while for the legacy of single-party rule to be overcome.

white minority rule

The early 1990s also saw the end of the last bastions of white minority rule in southern Africa – South Africa and Namibia – following the path taken by Zimbabwe in the 1980s. In South Africa itself, the system of apartheid had been deeply entrenched, with segregation between the races and denial of basic rights for the black majority enforced by the courts and the apparatus of the police state. The viability of the system was eroded during the 1980s through a combination of determined internal opposition, including armed struggle, and international sanctions.

The move to democracy with universal suffrage in 1994 was in many respects a textbook example of a negotiated transition between democratic forces and the representatives of the old

regime. After his release from twenty-seven years' imprisonment in
1990, Nelson Mandela became the key figure in a process of reconciliation between the African National Congress (ANC) and its former
oppressors. The eventual settlement comprised a model constitution, with an extensive bill of rights and a powerful constitutional
court; an all-party executive for five years, guaranteeing government
posts for the former ruling National Party, and a further guarantee
of security of jobs for five years to members of the civil service and
security forces. A Truth and Reconciliation Commission under
Archbishop Desmond Tutu offered immunity from prosecution to
former agents of the state who made a full acknowledgement of their
role in human rights violations committed under the apartheid
regime. Only extensive violence between supporters of the ANC and
the Inkatha Freedom Party in KwaZulu/Natal marred the successful
transition to democratic government in 1994.

However, the nature of the former regime and the struggle to
remove it have left significant legacies for the new democracy. At the
political level, the commanding position of the ANC and its affili-
ated organisations in leading the opposition to apartheid has left it
as the overwhelmingly dominant party in the new era, facing little
substantial competition from other parties. Much more serious has
been the economic and social legacy of apartheid. Whites own most
of the land and other productive assets. Over half of the majority
black population is living below the official poverty line, and suffers
from widespread unemployment, poor housing, health and education. Although there is a fast developing black middle class, the vast
majority are still awaiting the socio-economic improvements which
they expect democracy to deliver. Few commentators think South
Africa will follow the disastrous example of neighbouring
Zimbabwe. Yet that country stands as a warning of what can happen
when the economic settlement of the transition period unravels
under the pressure of resentment at white economic privilege and
their monopoly of fertile land.

from transition towards democratic consolidation

The four very different types of authoritarian regime reviewed here
have left quite different legacies for the electoral democracies that
have succeeded them. Military dictatorships, Communist systems,
African one-party states and white minority governments have produced widely differing problems of transition, and left very different

imprints on their successor regimes. Yet the further these countries have moved on from the initial period of transition in the early 1990s, the more we can detect a certain convergence between them in the problems they now confront in consolidating their democracies and in moving from a merely electoral form of democracy to a more substantial version which incorporates the different democratic components identified in chapter 2. Some countries may get stuck on the way in a hybrid form of regime. Understanding why this happens, and what the problems are with achieving a more robust form of democracy, will be reviewed in the next section.

consolidating and deepening democracy

The most striking difference between the development of democracy in the old democracies and the new or emerging ones is that of timescale. In most of the old democracies, the evolution towards their current democratic arrangements was a gradual one, spanning two centuries or more, and including some quite dramatic reverses. In most of the new democracies, only a decade or at most two have elapsed since the introduction of competitive elections marked a definitive break with authoritarian rule. It is hardly surprising, therefore, that progress towards a more developed and sustainable form of democracy should seem slow and halting, or even to have stalled altogether.

This is not just a question of timescale or longevity, however. We now realise that for a democratic system of government to prosper, it requires certain preconditions, which in the older democracies we have come to take for granted, but which may only be inadequately realised in the emerging democracies. For example, there has to be a functioning *state*, with an effective administration, whose writ runs throughout the territory. There has to be some minimum unity to the *nation*, as the basis for a common citizenship within agreed state borders. There has to be enough separation between the state and the majority *religion* to prevent religious bodies controlling the legislative and policy agenda. And there has to be a viable *economy*, growing over time and in a manner sufficient to meet some very basic needs and expectations of the citizens.

Now in the old democracies, these preconditions for democracy came to be established, and the conflicts associated with them largely resolved, prior to the development of electoral democracy. States were formed through conquest and dynastic alliance, and administrations established with a common language and law across the territory. In turn, these helped forge a sense of national identity among the population. The church came to be separated from the state, though in different degrees in different countries. And the enormous deprivations of the Industrial Revolution were endured before the vote was extended to the vast majority of the population, and while they were excluded from political influence. Democracy's preconditions, we could say, were established prior to the coming of democracy itself.

In the new democracies, by contrast, some of these preconditions may be only partially present. To the extent that this is so, then the challenge they face is not only one of developing a democracy, but of establishing some of its preconditions at the same time – and doing so under all the pressure of popular expectations and mobilisations, and intense rivalry between political parties and their leaderships. This is a much more difficult task than ever confronted the old democracies. It will be worth looking at each of these preconditions more closely: state, nation, religion, economy.

state

The most obvious precondition for democracy is that there should be a state which can enforce its law and administer its policy throughout its territory. This does not mean that the state should be excessively centralised. It may be a federal state, as India, Nigeria, Australia or the USA are, in which case the separate state governments should administer and enforce the law according to a constitutionally defined division of powers. Without this condition, however, the laws of a democratically elected legislature cannot have effect.

Some of the contexts where this condition of effective statehood is not met should be obvious: where there is civil war (as in Sierra Leone); where there is chronic insurgency (Angola) or warlordism (Afghanistan), or where significant parts of the territory are under the control of mafias or criminal organisations (Colombia). These are often described as 'broken-backed' states. In such conditions, democracy can have only a limited purchase, and it tends to be further undermined by the militarisation of the state that is involved in combating insurgency.

A less obvious but quite frequent condition is where the law enforcement agencies do not have the capacity or the will to enforce the law, or they do so in a manner that flagrantly and systematically exceeds their legal powers. In chapter 2, I mentioned the 'rule of law'. This is a double-sided idea: on one side, that the law should be not merely proclaimed but effectively enforced; on the other, that those responsible for its enforcement should themselves be subject to the law and act within their legally approved powers. Both are necessary if the basic rights of the citizen are to be protected. In the old democracies, this idea of the rule of law was well established *before* the advent of electoral democracy; without it, even electoral democracy can become a sham.

A further aspect of the state and its administration which we take for granted in the old democracies is the idea of the 'public interest'. Historians of the modern European state point to a key development when the finances of the state came to be separated from the personal finances of the monarch. From this, there gradually emerged the idea that the state and its administration existed to serve a public interest rather than the private interests of its office-holders. In particular, these were not expected to use their positions for personal enrichment, or to provide favours for family and friends. These norms took generations to establish, and were supported by the professionalisation of public administration during the nineteenth century, with full-time salaried posts, recruitment on merit and a predictable career structure. The same norms of public interest and public service also came to be accepted by elected politicians, albeit more slowly and patchily, after long periods when elected office was seen as a means to private enrichment and favouritism. These norms are now enshrined in a UN code of conduct for public officials.

Unfortunately, these norms are often honoured more in the breach than in the observance. In many countries corruption – the abuse of public office for private gain – is deeply ingrained, whether this takes the form of bribery for major public contracts, or routine greasing of the palm of officials for the performance of some basic service which they are officially employed to provide. Some of the causes are domestic, such as traditional norms which legitimate the powerful in maintaining a conspicuously different lifestyle from the ordinary citizen, and in using their position to benefit those with whom they have personal ties and obligations. In the case of lower officials, they may simply not be paid a living wage. Some causes are also external, such as collusion by foreign companies in order to beat their competitors to a lucrative public sector contract, which may be entirely inappropriate to the country's development needs. The

INTERNATIONAL CODE OF CONDUCT FOR PUBLIC OFFICIALS (SELECTED ARTICLES)

- A public office, as defined by national law, is a position of trust, implying a duty to act in the public interest. Therefore, the ultimate loyalty of public officials shall be to the public interest of their country as expressed through the democratic institutions of government.
- Public officials shall be attentive, fair and impartial in the performance of their functions and, in particular, in their relations with the public. They shall at no time afford any undue preferential treatment to any group or individual or improperly discriminate against any group or individual.
- Public officials shall not use their official authority for the improper advancement of their own or their family's personal or financial interest. They shall not engage in any transaction, acquire any position or function, or have any financial, commercial or other comparable interest that is incompatible with their office.
- Public officials shall not solicit or receive directly or indirectly any gift or other favours that may influence the exercise of their functions, performance of their duties or their judgement.

Source: UN Crime Prevention and Criminal Justice Division, 1997.

latest report of the major international 'corruption watch' non-governmental organisation, *Transparency International*, highlights the huge gulf between the developed and developing countries with respect to corruption: (see box opposite).

Whatever the combination of causes may be, corruption corrodes democracy because it inverts the proper relationship between rulers and ruled. Instead of politicians existing to serve the public, the public only exists to service the needs of politicians and their lifestyles. Elections on their own cannot solve this problem, if the idea of the public interest is only weakly developed. Indeed, they may simply reinforce it, as the costs of attaining electoral office put elected politicians under additional personal obligations which have to be met before the next round of elections comes. It is significant in this regard that political parties come top of the list in popular

TRANSPARENCY INTERNATIONAL CORRUPTION PERCEPTIONS INDEX, 2003

- This Index ranks the levels of corruption among politicians and public officials in 133 countries, as assessed by business people, academics and risk analysts, both within each country and outside. A score of ten indicates *no* corruption, a score of zero means *wholly* corrupt.
- The 2003 Index shows half of all developing countries scoring under three, indicating pervasive corruption, including such major countries as India (2.8), Russia (2.7), Indonesia (1.9) and Nigeria (1.4). Nine out of ten developing countries scored under five. At the other end of the scale, almost all developed countries scored above seven, with the exception of Italy (5.3) and Greece (4.3).
- In a parallel survey of the general public in forty-eight countries in 2003, the institutions held to be the most corrupt and most in need of reform were: political parties, the courts and the police.
- Another TI survey, the Bribe Payers Index, looked at the other side of the corruption relationship: the propensity of companies from top exporting countries to bribe in emerging markets. The survey found high levels of bribery by firms from Russia, China, Taiwan and South Korea, followed closely by Italy, Hong Kong, Malaysia, Japan, USA and France. Many of these countries have signed the OECD Anti-Bribery Convention, which outlaws bribery of foreign public officials. No successful prosecution has yet been brought under this convention.

(For further details, see: www.transparency.org)

perceptions of corrupt institutions, according to TI's survey of the public at large.

nation

In the old democracies, the perception of nationhood – of a people sharing a common identity through language, culture or shared history, and within broadly agreed borders – was established prior to the democratic era. In many of the new democracies, a sense of national identity is still rather tenuous. Especially in Africa and parts of Asia, the states that we have today were largely arbitrary creations of the colonial powers, and people shared loyalties across borders as much as within them. In addition, the divide-and-rule policies of the colonial powers intensified the differences between peoples inhabiting the same state.

Why does this matter? Democracy as rule by the people poses acutely the question: who constitutes 'the people'? And it presupposes a minimal level of agreement on who the people are who are to be subject to democratic decisions, and who are to share the equal rights and responsibilities of citizenship within a common state. If there is serious disagreement about this matter, it cannot be resolved through the operation of normal democratic procedures themselves, least of all by a simple majority vote. As the eighteenth-century democratic thinker Rousseau pointed out, before majority voting can be established, it requires *consensus* on its use, and on who the people are who are to be bound by its outcomes.

In the old democracies, the era of majority rule arrived with the question of nationhood already settled, though not to the same extent in all regions. Many new democracies, by contrast, are characterised by quite deep historical divisions of language, religion, culture or ethnicity, in comparison with which any sense of shared political identity or common citizenship is relatively weak. The nineteenth-century democratic thinker, John Stuart Mill, pointed to the disadvantage of this when he wrote that 'free institutions are next to impossible in a country made up of different nationalities', because 'each fears more injury to itself from other nationalities than from the common arbiter, the state'. Mill was doubtless being too categorical. Few states today contain a wholly homogeneous people; almost all are multi-cultural and multi-ethnic to a greater or lesser degree.

Yet the history of some of the new democracies shows that Mill's concerns were not fanciful. The transition to electoral democracy can itself serve to intensify pre-existing divisions within a country. This is partly because the coming of free expression and debate allows differences and antagonisms to be articulated that had previously been suppressed under authoritarian rule. More seriously, electoral competition encourages politicians to exploit those bases of popular support and mobilisation that will most readily deliver the numbers to ensure them political office. If the basis of such mobilisation lies in 'ethnic' or communal identities, then the electoral process can be enormously divisive. And the outcome can lead to inter-communal violence if one community becomes, or fears it will become, seriously disadvantaged by the advent of majority rule. In the worst cases, this can provoke ethnic cleansing and genocide, as happened in the former Yugoslavia.

So where the old democracies could take nationhood for granted as they democratised, many new ones have to develop democracy and a sense of national identity together in societies that may be deeply divided. This is not an impossible task, but it requires institutional arrangements which qualify the majoritarian, winner-take-all character of electoral competition, so that minority communities will not feel threatened by its outcome. Which arrangements are most appropriate for this purpose will depend on the context, and especially on whether the relevant minorities are territorially concentrated or dispersed.

Where minorities are concentrated, forms of regional autonomy may work by giving minorities a majority in their own regions, as in many federal states. Different faith communities may be allowed their own legal jurisdictions covering personal and family life, as in India. Other procedures may involve the requirement of electoral majorities that transcend ethnic or regional support, as in the rules for presidential elections in Kenya and Nigeria. Then there is the power-sharing executive, such as in the first years of South Africa's new constitution, already mentioned. Below these, there are quotas and other affirmative action programmes for government employment of all kinds. All such measures can be seen as different forms of power sharing, which ensure that the fate of minorities does not hang on the outcome of a single election. Democracy thus becomes a resource for the whole nation, not just for a section of it.

India provides the outstanding example of a country internally divided by religion, caste, language and region, which has nevertheless maintained a democratic government for over fifty years. It is of course not a 'new' democracy at all. As such, it offers a standing refutation to Mill's pessimistic conclusion about the incompatibility of democracy with deep communal divisions. Despite the dreadful legacy of ethnic cleansing that followed partition with Pakistan at independence in 1947, India is one of the very few post-colonial countries to have maintained democracy virtually unbroken since independence. Its different linguistic and territorial identities have been accommodated within the powerful regional states of the federation. The Congress Party, which ruled at the centre for a long time after independence, has been a pan-India party appealing across all communal divisions, rather than identifying with any one. And a long tradition of judicial independence has helped preserve the integrity of the constitution and respect for it. Inter-communal tensions still remain, especially between Hindus and Muslims in the disputed border region of Kashmir and elsewhere in North India. Also, the rise of a Hindu national party, the Bharatiya Janata Party, has been a disturbing development, though its record in coalition government has been more restrained than the exclusivist language of some of its supporters.

Despite such tensions, the history of India since independence offers some encouraging lessons for the preservation of democracy in divided or multi-cultural societies, over and above the need for the careful design of institutions. One is that people are capable of developing multi-level loyalties, to religion, region, ethnic or linguistic community, as well as to the nation as a whole. It is possible to sustain different identities without treating any one as exclusive of the others. And, secondly, the survival of democracy also depends on a certain exercise of self-restraint on the part of political leaders in the face of communal division, rather than a winner-take-all mentality which leaves groups feeling excluded, not just from government, but from democracy itself.

religion

A further precondition for democracy is that there should be a relative separation between Church or religion and the state. The old democracies entered the democratic era with the bitter conflicts over this question largely resolved, though in different ways in different countries. These different patterns refute one popular misconception about the relation between religion and democracy: that democracy requires a complete divorce between state and religion, i.e. that the state has to be thoroughly *secular*.

A secular state is prescribed in the constitutions of both France and the USA. In many European countries, however, there is an official state religion with an established church: Lutheran in Denmark, Finland and Norway, Anglican in England, and Orthodox in Greece. In the Netherlands and Germany, the state gives financial support to both Protestant and Catholic institutions. Even though such arrangements are now being questioned under the impetus of more multi-faith populations, they have not proved incompatible with democratic government.

What democracy requires with regard to religion is twofold. First, elected politicians and other state officials should not be subject to the control of any religious body, either formally or informally. Second, the state should not seek to impose the beliefs, rules or practices of one religion, even of the majority, on the followers of another, or discriminate against them in respect of citizenship rights. We could call these the principles of non-subordination and toleration respectively. It was the conflicts over these two principles which came to be settled in Western countries before the arrival of democratic politics, and resulted in what I have termed a 'relative' separation between Church and state, though not necessarily the absolute divorce, as in the secular constitutions of the USA and France.

Another common misconception about religion and democracy is the idea that some religions are by their very nature antipathetic to democracy. This is claimed, for example, by Samuel Huntington in his work with the apocalyptic title, *The Clash of Civilisations and the Remaking of World Order*. Yet none of the major world religions has in practice been monolithic. Their core doctrines have usually been subject to a variety of schools of interpretation, and with the selective reading of texts they have all been used to justify a range of different political orders, according to circumstances. Thus, Christianity has historically supported both the divine right of kings and the most egalitarian republicanism. Confucianism today is aligned behind the democracies of Taiwan and South Korea, and is also appealed to for justification of Singapore's authoritarian regime in the name of 'Asian values'.

The same diversity applies to Islam, despite widespread assumptions to the contrary. Just as many Muslims in the world live in electoral democracies as under authoritarian regimes: in Bangladesh, India, Indonesia, Nigeria and Turkey, to name the largest five. In three of these five, Muslims are in the overwhelming majority. In these, religion plays an important part in civil society, through welfare and educational institutions, but not in the state itself, where the two principles mentioned above are respected.

So why is the misconception about Islam's incompatibility with democracy so prevalent? This is mainly because of the emergence of a militantly anti-Western theocratic regime in Iran following the revolution of 1979, and the development of Islamist movements throughout the Arab world demanding a confessional state with the strict imposition of Islamic canon law, or sharia. In Iran, the Western-backed shah was deposed in the revolution of 1979 and replaced by a novel form of theocracy under the Ayatollah Khomeini. In this 'Islamic Republic' sovereignty lies with God, whose commands are interpreted by a clerical Supreme Leader, assisted by a religious Council of Guardians. These Guardians enjoy a veto power over all laws and candidates for elected legislative office, and control the courts and security services. If the people threaten to elect liberalising reformers to parliament, as they regularly do, their candidates are simply vetoed, as happened most recently in 2004. Although the regime sometimes describes itself as an Islamic democracy, in practice it is no more democratic than the 'people's democracies' of the Soviet era, in which the will of the proletariat could only be truly known by the guardians of Communist orthodoxy.

The example of the Iranian theocracy encouraged the development of fundamentalist Islamist movements across the Arab world, even where the regime did not actively sponsor them. These movements have found a ready following among the impoverished urban youth, and ready-made grievances against their own Western supported regimes, and against Israeli oppression of the Palestinians. Most have had active terrorist wings, which have invited repression in turn from their governments, thus reinforcing a cycle of authoritarianism throughout the region.

Could such a movement ever come to power if free electoral competition were allowed? Just such a possibility seemed on the cards in Algeria in 1991, after a new constitution had brought to an end the one-party state under the National Liberation Front. In the subsequent elections, a radical Islamist party called the Islamic Salvation Front was set to become the largest party in the National Assembly after the first round of elections. Before the second round could take place, however, the army intervened to cancel them, and banned the party from politics altogether. This action initiated almost a decade of violent conflict between the military-backed regime and radical Islamists, in which more than a hundred thousand people lost their lives.

The Algerian example has added further credence to the idea that Islam and democracy are incompatible. It has also resurrected an old democratic conundrum in modern guise: can the electoral process be used to bring an end to democracy? If so, what should be the appropriate democratic response? This precise question was put to the test in Turkey in 1997, when the military-backed constitutional court ordered the disbandment of the largest party in Parliament –

the Islamic Welfare Party – and its removal from the coalition government. The grounds given were that some of the party's leaders were on record as having advocated the introduction of sharia law for Turkey's Muslim majority, which would yield power to extra-parliamentary and extra-judicial religious bodies, in contravention of Turkey's secular constitution. No such measure had been introduced by the party in government itself, but the court decided to take no chances.

Were they right to do so? The Welfare Party appealed to the European Court of Human Rights at Strasbourg on the grounds that their freedom of association had been violated by the court's decision. So the question of Turkish democracy's future came to be decided by an international human rights court.

THE EUROPEAN COURT OF HUMAN RIGHTS DECIDES

- One group of judges maintained that Turkey's constitutional court had been justified in its ban. 'There can be no democracy', they argued, 'where the people of a state, even by majority decision, waive their legislative and judicial powers in favour of an entity which is not responsible to the people it governs.' In other words, democracy had to be curtailed in the present in order to preserve it in the future; in effect, the people had to be protected from the consequences of their own electoral decisions.
- The other group of judges maintained that the party's freedom of association had been violated. 'Democracy is meaningless,' they argued, 'without the free expression of electoral opinion ... and this requires the participation of a plurality of political parties representing different shades of opinion, even those that call into question the way the state is organised.' In other words, democracy requires that all views be publicly aired and resolved through discussion, not suppressed.
- The court found in favour of the ban on the Welfare Party by four votes to three.

Source: Council of Europe, *Case of Refah Partisi and others v. Turkey*, 31 July 2001.

Fortunately, the outcome in Turkey was nothing like as disastrous as in Algeria. A new Islamic party was formed to take the place of the banned one, but with an explicit rejection of the Islamist agenda, and a commitment to promoting Turkey's membership of the European Union. It proceeded to win an overwhelming majority in the election of 2002. This outcome confirms that not only Islam but even a confessedly Islamic party is quite compatible with democracy, just as Christian Democratic parties have been in Catholic Europe. Yet there must remain a concern that in the much more fraught context of the Arab world, the advent of a truly free electoral democracy would bring the issue of the relation between religion and the state directly onto the political agenda once more, in a way that might jeopardise democracy's survival.

economy

The most striking difference between the old and new democracies is that the former belong almost exclusively to the developed industrial world, and the latter mainly to the developing economies of the South. In the former, the huge shocks and deprivations of the Industrial Revolution in the nineteenth century took place while the working classes were still excluded from the vote. It was only when their economies had grown sufficiently to be able to meet some of the demands of organised labour, and deliver free primary education, that the vote came to be extended to the whole population. The history of the twentieth century was one of the working classes using the vote they had won to moderate the inequalities and unpredictabilities of market capitalism through social insurance, redistributive taxation and the other institutions of the welfare state. Democratic procedures gained support, in other words, by people being able to see the results in their daily lives.

Most people do not understand democracy in merely political terms. They expect their exercise of the vote to produce policies that will improve their economic conditions and meet basic needs, such as those for clean water, sanitation, health care, housing and education. When democratic governments repeatedly fail to meet the minimal expectations of their electorates, the result is disillusionment and apathy, or, in the worst cases, vulnerability to capture by extremist political movements. The large-scale and chronic unemployment created by the worldwide economic slump in the

1920s and 1930s pushed the more insecure democracies of that time into the hands of fascism and other forms of authoritarianism.

This very simplified account serves to make an obvious point. The fate of democratic institutions cannot be divorced from the economic context in which they are placed, or from the economic expectations that accompany people's achievement of the vote. With a few exceptions, such as the east Asian countries of Taiwan and South Korea, most of the new democracies are not only economically undeveloped compared with the old; in many respects, they are also at a lower level of economic development than the old democracies were when they introduced universal suffrage. Not only that, but their prospects for development are conditioned by the pattern of their relations with the economically developed North. They are part of the same competitive global market, whose terms of engagement are largely set by the developed countries themselves. It will be useful to itemise some of the key features of this economic context in which the new democracies operate, and which are relevant to their longer-term democratic viability.

underdevelopment

It has long been an accepted tenet of political science that sustained economic development is advantageous to democratic consolidation. There are a number of reasons for this. Economic development increases employment opportunities and limits concentrations of the jobless and disaffected, especially in urban centres. Over time, it generates intermediate technical and professional strata, whose conditions of life and work incline them to defend democratic freedoms. And it gives governments economic room to finance improvements in health and education, which develop the human resources necessary to further both economic development and the working of democracy itself. By the same token, retarded development, or economic growth which only benefits a small minority, is a handicap. In most of sub-Saharan Africa, to take the most disadvantaged region, economic conditions have not improved at all for the vast majority during the 1980s and 1990s, and the blight of AIDS has led to sharp reductions in life expectancy. Figure 4.1 on page 79 charts both the absolute decline in per capita Gross Domestic Product (GDP) in the region and its relative decline in comparison with other regions. According to World Bank figures, where the per capita GDP of the twenty richest countries in the world was eighteen times that of the twenty poorest in 1960, by 1995 this had increased to thirty-seven times.

indebtedness

All developing countries need to borrow from abroad to finance essential development projects, and they borrow both from commercial banks and from international institutions, such as the World Bank and the regional development banks. However, many of the countries that made the transition to electoral democracy in the 1980s and 1990s did so with a potentially unsustainable burden of debt repayments, due to a combination of high interest rates, economically unproductive projects and a decline in the value of their currency and export earnings relative to the dollar. Included in these repayments was debt incurred by former dictators to finance prestige projects, military spending, lavish personal lifestyles and overseas bank accounts.

Zambia represents an extreme case of an African country where, throughout the 1990s, debt servicing consumed thirty per cent of government expenditure, far more than it spent on basic social services, such as health and education. In South America, where levels of indebtedness are the highest in the world, Argentina was brought to the verge of economic collapse in 2001–2 by its inability to fund debt repayments. Unemployment soared; the value of savings and pensions plummeted; bank withdrawals had to be suspended, and three different presidents lost office within the space of a month under the pressure of mass demonstrations. Some commentators regard the fact that no military coup took place, as it would have done under similar conditions in the past, as evidence of the consolidation of Argentina's democracy. Yet with half the population reduced to living below the poverty line, public confidence in democratic institutions remains extremely fragile.

IMF conditionality

When countries get into difficulties with their debt repayments, or face a currency crisis brought on by international speculation, their only resort is to the International Monetary Fund (IMF) for a bailout. They are then required to submit to externally imposed conditions, which follow standard free-market prescriptions: devaluation of the currency, privatisation of state enterprises, reduction in welfare spending, introduction of payment for basic health care and education, and a shift of the economy to export production. Countries which have no oil or mineral wealth are then caught in a double bind. The export goods in which they have most competitive

TWO LEADING US ECONOMIC FIGURES REFLECT ON THE GLOBAL ECONOMIC SYSTEM

- 'Trade liberalization all too often fails to live up to its promise ... Western countries pushed trade liberalization for the products they exported, but at the same time continued to protect those sectors in which competition from developing countries might have threatened their economies.' 'If IMF policies had simply failed to accomplish the full potential of development, that would have been bad enough. But the failures in many places have set back the development agenda.' Joseph Stiglitz, Nobel Laureate in Economics, 2001, and former economist at the World Bank.
- 'Financial markets are inherently unstable and the playing field is inherently uneven ... emerging market economies are suffering from capital outflows *and* higher borrowing costs.' 'The critics are right in claiming that the World Trade Organization is biased in favor of the rich countries and multinational corporations.' George Soros, international financier and philanthropist.

Source: J. Stiglitz, *Globalization and its Discontents*. G. Soros, *On Globalization*.

advantage – agriculture and textiles – are the very ones where the free market is rigged by the farm subsidy and tariff protection regimes maintained by the developed countries to support their own producers. It has been calculated that the cost of these regimes to developing country producers far exceeds the total value of the international development aid advanced by the developed countries.

inequality

As I have already argued, sustainable democracy and equal citizenship can coexist with *economic* inequality, provided the potentially distorting effects of that on the democratic process are contained. Yet the greater the economic inequality, the more difficult that containment is. With the typically high levels of inequality between rich and poor in developing countries, it is difficult for the rich to consider the deprived as equal citizens with themselves. They tend to shut themselves away in privately guarded enclaves, and they regard their peer group as the élites of the developed world, not their own

Table 4.4　Inequality of income in selected countries during the 1990s*

| | Gini Index | Most unequal | |
| | | Percentage share of national income | |
		Top 20%	Bottom 20%
Sierra Leone	62.9	63.4	1.1
South Africa	59.3	64.8	2.9
Brazil	59.1	63.0	2.6

Other countries over GI 55: Argentina, Bolivia, Chile, Colombia, Guatemala, Guinea Bissau, Honduras, Nicaragua, Paraguay, Zimbabwe

| | Gini Index | Percentage share of national income | |
		Top 20%	Bottom 20%
Russia	48.7	53.7	4.4
USA	40.8	46.4	5.2
UK	36.1	43.0	6.6

Countries on GI 25 and under: Belgium, Czech Republic, Finland, Japan, Norway, Sweden

| | Gini Index | Most equal | |
| | | Percentage share of national income | |
		Top 20%	Bottom 20%
Denmark	24.7	34.5	9.6
Hungary	24.4	34.4	10.0
Slovakia	19.5	31.4	11.9

Source: *The World Guide, 2003/4*, drawn from World Bank 2001 *World Development Indicators 2001.*

* The Gini Index measures the degree of a country's inequality on a scale of 0 to 100, where 0 represents perfect equality and 100 the most extreme inequality. What these figures mean in practical terms can be seen by comparing the percentage of a country's income accruing to the top 20% and bottom 20% respectively of a country's population.

countrymen. At the same time, they tend to be the strata from which the political leaderships of their countries are drawn, and, once elected, will most likely give priority to the needs of their own kind rather than to the poor. This explains the phenomenon of 'élite capture', whereby a political leadership can be replaced through the electoral process without much noticeable benefit for the mass of the population.

Table 4.4 shows comparative levels of inequality for countries at the top and bottom of the inequality index, with the USA, UK and Russia for comparison. Almost all the countries with the greatest inequality are to be found in Latin America, where there have long existed huge concentrations of private ownership of land and economic enterprises. A similar pattern is to be found in the former white colonies of South Africa and Zimbabwe. At the other end of the scale, almost all the countries of greatest equality are to be found in continental Europe, with its history of left-wing parties, Social Democrat or Communist, using political power to redistribute wealth.

While few would now advocate a return to Communist rule, the message from the European experience is clear. The only way to moderate the systematic inequalities of a market economy, compounding historic ownership patterns, is by government policies which have a consciously redistributive effect. Yet these are now more difficult to achieve than before. Not only do the wealthy have more sophisticated means to evade taxation. The need to keep the support of the international financial community, discussed in the previous chapter, bears even more heavily on the developing countries than on the developed ones. Brazil is a key test case here. In October 2002, the Workers Party swept to power on a redistributive agenda, with a former trade unionist, Lula da Silva, elected as president. Yet, having inherited the highest debt service to export ratio of any country in the world, at over one hundred per cent, his first priority has had to be to satisfy international creditors with the soundness of his fiscal policies. And redistribution does not come high on their agenda.

conclusion

Since this has been a long section, it will be helpful if I summarise its themes in a few simple points:

1. Electoral democracy, that is the election of a government by universal suffrage with freedoms of association and expression, constitutes the beginning, not the end-point, of democracy. It requires much more to realise a society of politically equal citizens, living under the rule of law, who are genuinely able to influence

government policies in their interests, which is what democracy promises. Without the realisation of this promise, electoral democracy can be merely a form without substance.

2. The old democracies have taken a considerable span of time to reach towards this goal, with some notable reverses. They entered the era of mass democracy with many of its facilitating conditions already established in a pre-democratic age. By and large, they had effectively functioning states, subject to the rule of law and observing a norm of public interest. Disputes over nationhood and the relation between religion and the state had been largely settled. Moreover, they were already set on the path of economic and industrial development. The difficult task confronting the new democracies, by contrast, is how to consolidate and develop democracy in the absence of some, if not all, of these conditions, which have therefore to be achieved simultaneously with the working of democratic procedures and institutions.

3. The international context is both a help and a hindrance to this project. Of great help are international public norms supportive of democracy and human rights, combined with specific assistance from Western governments in helping develop democratic institutions. Against this has to be set a global economic and financial structure which works to the disadvantage of developing economies and their producers, and according to radical free-market norms which penalise the kind of redistributive policies that many of the old democracies found necessary to consolidate public support for their own democratic institutions. These and other features of the international order will be treated more fully in the following chapter.

further reading

Chua, Amy. *World on Fire*. New York: Random House, 2003.

Democratization (quarterly journal on democracy). London: Frank Cass.

Hadenius, Axel. *Democracy's Victory and Crisis*. Cambridge: Cambridge University Press, 1997.

Journal of Democracy (quarterly journal on democracy). Baltimore: Johns Hopkins University Press.

Linz, Juan and Alfred Stepan. *Problems of Democratic Transition and Consolidation*. Baltimore: Johns Hopkins University Press, 1996.

Markoff, John. *Waves of Democracy*. London and Thousand Oaks CA: Sage Publications, 1996.

Mill, John Stuart. *Representative Government*. London: Dent, 1910.

Sen, Amartya. *Development as Freedom*. New York: Alfred Knopf; Oxford: Oxford University Press, 1999.

Sorensen, Georg. *Democracy and Democratization*. Boulder and San Francisco: Westview Press, 1993.

Soros, George. *On Globalization*. Oxford and New York: Public Affairs, 2002.

Stiglitz, Joseph. *Globalization and its Discontents*. London: Allen Lane; New York: Norton, 2002.

globalising democracy

This chapter will consider a number of critical contemporary issues around the theme of global democracy. The first section will examine the policies developed by Western governments since the 1980s to help promote democracy and human rights around the world. What is their rationale? How successful have they been? Can democracy be exported? The second section will consider key issues of democracy at the global level. Can international institutions be democratised, and, if so, how? What place is there in this for a global civil society? Can globalisation be made to work for peoples as well as for corporations and financiers? The final section will look at debates about the 'democratic deficit' in the European Union, as a test case for democratisation at the international level. Can the EU ever become more democratic?

democracy promotion

Since the late 1980s, Western governments have made the promotion and support of democracy in previously non-democratic countries an important part of their foreign and international aid policies. This was not always so. During the Cold War their priority was to prevent the spread of Communism, and they were quite prepared to give support to dictators who were anti-Communist or who in other ways aligned themselves with Western strategic and economic interests. Over this period, there were also notorious cases where the USA in particular worked actively to undermine democratic governments whose programme was perceived to be

too left-wing: in Iran in 1953, in Chile in 1973, and in Nicaragua
after the Sandinistas had won open elections in 1984.

With the fall of Soviet Communism at the end of the 1980s, these
priorities changed. Not only had Western-style democracy proved to
be almost the only serious contender for people's allegiance left
holding the field internationally, but also the collapse of a socialist
alternative economic model reinforced the dominance of a radical
free-market ideology as a global norm for economic policy, including the policies of the main international financial institutions. It
was now unlikely that democratisation would bring to power
political parties which might threaten private property or Western
economic interests. Indeed, democracy and the free market were
seen as intimately linked and mutually reinforcing.

There was also a strategic reason for an active policy of democracy promotion. Evidence suggested that democracies did not go to
war against one another. They might, and often did, go to war
against authoritarian regimes. But they did not attack each other.
The spread of democracy, therefore, would increase international
security, as well as help protect the peoples concerned from the
worst human rights abuses.

Did this agenda simply represent another export of Western
cultural values to the non-Western world? There are good grounds
for believing, as I have already argued in chapter 1, that the assumptions on which democratic principles are grounded have a universal
applicability. Despite all the cultural differences between people,
there are certain common characteristics which we all share. There
are common human *needs*, for subsistence, security and respect.
There are shared *capacities* for reflective moral and political choice.
There are also common human *limitations*, or failings, such as
limited knowledge and a tendency for the exercise of power to go to
rulers' heads. It is the common needs that make democracy
desirable, the shared capacities that make it *possible*, and the all-
too-human limitations that make it *necessary*. If this reasoning is
correct, then it must be as applicable in Beijing or Jakarta as in Paris,
London or Washington. Good arguments do not stop at borders.

The same applies to the typical democratic institutions, outlined
in chapter 2, which have proved necessary to subject the modern
state to a measure of popular control with inclusive citizenship.
Although these institutions may have evolved in the West, now that
the modern state form has become generalised across the world,
these institutions have come to have an exemplary significance for

democracies everywhere. Naturally, there may be as many variations upon them in practice as exist among Western democracies themselves, and new forms suited to local conditions will always be experimented with. In this sense, neither the Washington nor the Westminster variants can be prescriptive.

At the same time, it is not just a question of the *arguments* for democracy having a universal reach. It is also that, as a matter of fact, democratic ideas have proved attractive to people in every society across the world – and they have shown themselves prepared to struggle to achieve them. It is only because of this domestic support for democratic ideas that the efforts of Western governments to promote democracy have had any impact upon other countries, and the impact has usually been proportionate to the extent and depth of that domestic commitment. In a number of countries, the external leverage applied by Western governments may well have brought a transition from authoritarian rule to free elections sooner than would otherwise have occurred.

Nevertheless, there are a number of reasons why the actual *practice* of democracy promotion by Western governments over the past decade or so should have seemed more like a distinctively Western rather than a truly international agenda. Let me give just some of these reasons:

- External involvement in the internal politics of another country can be quite intrusive, and appear as an infringement of the country's sovereignty, especially when carried out by a former imperial power. Although it is now internationally accepted that intervention in a country may be justified to prevent the worst human rights abuses, how this should be done and by whom remains controversial, and in any case democracy promotion goes beyond this purely preventative purpose.
- Democracy promotion has rarely been applied consistently, since it has always had to compete with a government's other foreign policy goals, including its strategic and economic interests. Western governments have been ready to abandon pressure for democratisation when these other considerations intervened, creating an impression of double standards rather than principled commitment.
- The linkage drawn by Western governments between political democratisation and radical liberalisation of the economy, to the point where they are seen as virtually interchangeable, has tended

to pre-empt or restrict possible policy options for a newly elected government by what are seen as Western priorities. In some cases, as I pointed out in the previous chapter, it has weakened popular support for the democratic process.

These points are worth exploring further by examining three different modes of democracy promotion that have been adopted since 1990: political conditionality, democracy assistance, and now, in Iraq, democratisation through armed invasion.

political conditionality

Political conditionality involves attaching conditions to aid, trade or other benefits, in order to encourage progress towards democracy or improvements in a country's human rights record. During the 1980s, public opinion in Western countries became increasingly critical of government aid being advanced to authoritarian and corrupt regimes, and attaching conditions to its continuation fitted well with the new democratising agenda. Such conditionality proved most effective in moving reluctant regimes towards free elections where it was combined with significant internal pressures, and where the regime was particularly vulnerable to aid or trade sanctions. Examples include Malawi (1992–3) and Kenya (1991–3) in Africa and Haiti (1991–4) in Central America. In other countries, such as Guatemala (1993) and Peru (1992), sanctions were used to prevent a reversion to non-constitutional rule.

However, in countries where the West has had strong commercial or strategic interests, sanctions have proved either half-hearted or non-existent. Western countries continued to give aid to the oppressive regime of Suharto in Indonesia throughout the 1990s until it fell in 1998. China has proved too important a trading partner for any sanctions to be more than temporary and token. Aid conditionality imposed on Nigeria after it reverted to military rule in 1993 was half-hearted. Limited sanctions imposed after the military coup in Pakistan in 1999 were lifted to ensure the government's strategic support in the war against the Taliban. Egypt continues to be the second largest recipient of US aid after Israel, despite being a de facto one-party state with substantial internal repression. Saudi Arabia's corrupt and repressive monarchy has always been courted by Western governments because of their dependence on its oil exports and arms purchases. And so on.

Now, in many of these cases it can be argued that Western governments were unlikely to have much influence in changing internal political conditions anyway. And the promotion of a country's commercial interests has always been a perfectly legitimate goal of foreign policy. Yet the inconsistencies in the treatment of different countries in practice has inevitably led to the charge of double standards, and has significantly eroded the moral authority of Western governments as international defenders of democracy and human rights. The collapse of the British Labour Government's much vaunted 'ethical foreign policy' is a classic example of the problem of maintaining any consistency of ethical stance in this complex policy field, when consistency is precisely what is required for credibility.

The one region where political conditionality has been most consistently successful has been in Europe. Here, the candidate countries for membership of the European Union from Eastern/Central Europe have had to meet quite stringent political conditions for joining the 'club'. The expected economic benefits of membership have provided a very powerful incentive for the applicant countries to agree to annual audits of their progress in improving key aspects of their democratic practice, such as the rule of law, the treatment of minorities and protection for civil and political rights. Although other regions of the world do not have organisations to match the EU, the model it offers of regional bodies to support democratisation in their own region is likely to prove more effective and acceptable in the long run than intervention from outside the region. This showed itself, for example, in Latin America, where the reversal of the coup in Venezuela in 2002 owed much to pressure from within the region, although the coup had been welcomed by the US government.

democracy assistance

Sanctions of any kind are a very blunt instrument, and tend only to work where the intended outcome is clear-cut, such as the introduction of competitive elections, or reversing a slide back to authoritarian rule. For the much more complex processes involved in consolidating and deepening democracy once electoral democracy is in place, positive assistance with specifically targeted programmes is a much more appropriate means of democracy promotion. Since 1990, Western governments have devoted an increasing proportion of development aid to what is called 'capacity building': training legislators, electoral commissioners, ombudsmen, community policemen, and so on. Considerable assistance has also gone to fund non-governmental organisations (NGOs), which are seen as having a key role to play in the defence of citizens' rights and in holding governments to societal account. Democracy is not cheap, and impoverished countries particularly need outside help and resources in its development.

However, two problems are recurrent in this kind of assistance. The first is that even well-meaning programmes can be politically intrusive. Governments by their nature do not welcome public scrutiny or effective opposition, and assistance designed to improve the quality of both may lead donor governments to appear to be taking sides politically. Channelling official aid through democracy foundations or human rights organisations does not entirely remove this dilemma. Secondly, many NGOs in developing countries have come to be entirely dependent on external funding for their activities, rather than being resourced by contributions from their own membership. As such, they hardly meet the criteria of self-organisation and self-sustainability which are supposedly necessary for a democratic civil society. Again, the poverty of domestic resources is to blame. Yet it exemplifies a tension within the whole project of democracy promotion. If democracy means people taking responsibility for the running of their own affairs, then there is a certain contradiction in this being so dependent on initiatives and resources from outside.

democratisation by armed invasion

Nowhere is this contradiction more evident than in the attempt to bring democracy to a country by armed invasion – to promote a people's self-determination through a systematic violation of it – as in Iraq. Whatever the public reasons that were subsequently given to justify the US and UK invasion of Iraq, it is now clear that the original purpose lay in an ambitious project long harboured by the neo-conservative group around President Bush. This involved nothing short of a radical transformation of the Middle East by the removal of Saddam Hussein and the installation of a democratic regime in his place that would have a domino effect on the other authoritarian regimes of the region. The example they appealed to was the successful introduction of democracy in West Germany and Japan by the victors at the end of the Second World War.

However, these precedents were historically unique in the sheer scale and duration of the war which the two countries had unleashed, and the corresponding international legitimacy which accompanied the victors' project for reconstruction. As a model for Iraq, they have proved highly misleading. In contrast to them, Iraq – and, in a lesser manner, Afghanistan, which preceded it – has demonstrated the acute contradictions of imposing democracy on a country by force of arms, however much people both inside and outside the country may have welcomed the end of a tyrannical regime. This is because of a number of factors that armed invasion and occupation necessarily bring with them, which work against any programme for democratisation, and which were revealed most acutely in the year after the fall of Saddam.

* Invasion brings the collapse of the existing state apparatus, which produces a vacuum at three levels simultaneously – security, administration and politics. The indigenous personnel being trained to fill this vacuum become identified as agents of the occupying powers and as themselves targets for resistance.
* Invasion produces a radical shift in the balance of forces between the different communities making up the country, and a legacy of resentment on the part of those losing out, which can endanger an already fragile sense of nationhood.
* There is an acute legitimacy–security conundrum. Because the regime created after the invasion is widely perceived to lack legitimacy, it provokes resistance and intensifies insecurity, while the means used to deal with resistance only further delegitimate the regime. At the same time, the one political process that would provide legitimacy for a government, national elections, have to be postponed because of the continuing insecurity.
* The policy agenda of the invaders comes to pre-empt and set limits to whatever indigenous democratisation process might eventually emerge: for example, the privatisation of industry, the indefinite stationing of foreign troops, a pro-Western foreign policy, and so on.
* The timetable of any democratisation that takes place is not set by the requirements of an indigenous process, but by the domestic imperatives and electoral timetable of the occupying power.

> It would be impossible for the US to expend such massive human and material resources here and then allow any regime that isn't in their interests. The Americans want influence and a strong ally. The Iraqis want their own government. (Mohammed al-Askari)

Although at the time of writing it is too soon to make any final judgement on the Iraq experiment, its record to date reveals in the most acute form the contradictions intrinsic to much democracy promotion: between the democratic requirement of a country's genuine self-determination, and the economic and strategic interests of the democracy-promoting powers. Such contradictions are almost unavoidable if the agenda of democracy promotion becomes the preserve of individual states, as it largely has been, rather than of regional or international institutions representing a wider international community. How far such institutions can themselves be arenas for democratic practice or democracy promotion will be the subject of the following sections.

democratising global institutions

In chapter 3 I raised a central paradox of democratic government today. This is that the institutions of representative democracy were designed to enable the popular control of government at the level of the national state, but that many of the forces which affect the well-being of citizens are beyond the state's control. What value is there in the popular control of government if the government itself does not control what matters for the lives of its citizens?

Some of these external determinants are located in other states. Their civil wars produce an influx of refugees; their activities pollute our rivers or restrict our water supply; their decision to devalue the currency affects our economic competitiveness; the subsidies to their producers ruin the livelihoods of our own. Some of these factors are located in the international market and its key operators, which determine the price of oil and other raw materials, or the access of countries and their businesses to credit, or can generate a run on a country's currency. And some are the unintended consequences of human activity across the world: global warming, with its increase in extreme weather events; depletion of fish stocks and other natural resources; pollution of the atmosphere and the seas; the transmission of epidemics, such as AIDS.

Now the standard instrument for addressing these problems that spill over state borders is through international organisations created by treaty agreement between states. The international scene is crowded with such organisations, most of them offshoots of the United Nations, such as the International Monetary Fund (IMF), the

World Bank, or the World Trade Organisation (WTO) in the economic field, or the World Food Programme or the World Health Organisation in the social field. These organisations make rules and decisions which are binding on states, in ways that can affect their citizens' lives. Yet in many respects these organisations are not themselves particularly democratic in the way they take their decisions; so the focus of proposals for democratisation at the international level has come to centre on these organisations.

From the perspective of developing countries in particular, the problem with many of the key international organisations is that their decision-making structures are weighted towards the major powers in the developed world, and their policies correspondingly serve their interests. This is true of the big four: the UN Security Council, the IMF, the World Bank and the WTO. Governments which are at the receiving end of IMF 'structural adjustment' programmes, for example, experience it as another external imposition over which they have little control, rather than as the legitimate product of treaty agreements into which they have entered voluntarily.

From a broader democratic point of view, the problem with these international organisations lies not just in the imbalance of power and representation between states by which they operate. It is that they act as the agents of *states*, and not necessarily of *peoples*. A number of the member states are not democratic themselves. Even those that are have grossly inadequate mechanisms for subjecting their representatives on these organisations to any democratic accountability, whether to national legislatures, or to public opinion. Decision making at the international level is mainly a matter of bargaining in secret between self-enclosed élites or policy experts, acting 'in the interests of state', from which the people are largely absent. It is such characteristics that have fuelled demands for greater democratisation at the international level.

Before examining some of the proposals put forward, it will be worth considering at the outset two frequent objections made to the whole idea of democratising global institutions. One is a crude power consideration. Their undemocratic features, it is argued, such as the veto of permanent members of the UN Security Council, were designed precisely to keep the major powers involved, and to prevent them simply ignoring the organisations and rendering them ineffective, as happened to the League of Nations in the 1930s. Yet this cannot be a decisive objection to at least sketching out what a more democratic international organisation could or should look like, and mobilising support behind it. Even the USA in its unilateralist mode under President Bush has found that it cannot do without organisations such as the UN. And few countries except France and the UK can support an arrangement of Security Council voting which was fixed in stone by the power configurations at the end of the Second World War. In any case, if democratic principles are now claimed to have universal scope, why should international institutions be excluded from their application?

A second objection is more substantial. This contends that dimensions of scale make democracy unrealisable at the global level. Any popular control will be so attenuated as to be virtually meaningless. This dilemma has been well expressed by the US democratic theorist, Robert Dahl:

> A smaller democratic unit provides an ordinary citizen with greater opportunities to participate in government than a larger one. But the smaller the unit the more likely that some matters of importance to the citizen are beyond the capacity of the government to deal with effectively. To handle these broader matters, the democratic unit might be enlarged; but in doing so the capacity of the citizen to participate effectively in governing would be diminished. (Dahl, in Shapiro, ed.)

At the global level, this capacity is reduced to zero. In addition, Dahl argues, the differences of interest and values between people would become so great at that level that they would be beyond the scope of any democratic decisional mechanism to resolve. The least bad solution, he concludes, would seem to be the system of bargaining between expert policy élites which we already have.

The validity of Dahl's objections cannot be seriously assessed until we have considered some actual proposals for global democratisation. Two different types of proposal will be considered. The first, more modest, keeps the existing intergovernmental or state-centred structure of the international organisations, but explores how they might be made more representative, accountable and transparent. A second, more ambitious, type of proposal argues for a much greater range of actors to be involved in the decision making of international organisations besides states: civil society organisations, people's representatives, municipalities and others. After considering these proposals, we shall be in a better position to decide how far Dahl's objections hold up.

a minimalist agenda for democratisation

To get a clearer idea of what is involved in this first type of proposal, it will be best to start with a brief thumbnail sketch of the four most important intergovernmental organisations.

IMPORTANT INTERGOVERNMENTAL ORGANISATIONS

the united nations

The UN was founded at the end of the Second World War to promote international peace and security, human rights and social development. All internationally recognised states are members. The General Assembly is the main deliberative body, composed of permanent representatives of all member states, each of whom has one vote. Decisions on the most important questions require a two-thirds majority, but the Assembly has no power to enforce its decisions. The only body whose decisions are binding on member states is the Security Council, made up of five permanent members (China, France, Russia, the UK and USA) and ten temporary members elected by the General Assembly. The five permanent members, all nuclear weapons states, have a veto over any Security Council resolution, including proposals for constitutional change of the UN. They are also not above using their economic muscle to get their way, by pressurising non-permanent members, or withholding financial contributions to the organisation as a whole. To put the cost of the UN in perspective, the annual expenditure of the organisation and all its subsidiary bodies is equivalent to the sum spent every thirty-six hours by the US Pentagon.

international monetary fund

The IMF is part of the UN family of organisations. It was established in 1944 in the aftermath of the Great Depression to maintain global economic stability by providing loans to countries facing economic slump or balance of payments problems, and generally ensuring conditions for global economic growth. Although almost all states are members, their voting power is proportionate to the amount of capital they provide to the Fund. The eight 'G8' developed nations control almost half the total votes, and each has a director on the executive board, while the other sixteen directors are elected by the remaining 165 member states, grouped in regional constituencies. The managing director is always a European, and his deputy a North American.

Not surprisingly, given this structure, the policies of the Fund reflect the financial orthodoxies and interests of the developed world and their banks. When these shifted in the 1980s in a radical free-market direction, the Fund became a global champion of market supremacy, imposing contractionary policies on debtor countries which served to plunge them even further into debt.

the world bank (international bank for reconstruction and development)

The World Bank is a parallel organisation to the IMF, with a similar arrangement of voting weighted according to financial contribution from member states, and a president who is always a US citizen nominated by the US Treasury Secretary. Its purpose is more development oriented than the IMF, and it provides loans and expertise for development projects, as well as adjustment loans to help countries pay their debts. Although its policy stance shifted during the 1990s towards requiring 'poverty reduction strategies' from debtor governments, its overall framework of neo-liberal market orthodoxy has proved no more conducive to debt reduction in the developing world than the policies of the IMF.

the world trade organisation

The WTO was established in 1994 from the former General Agreement on Tariffs and Trade (GATT). Its purpose is to encourage the expansion of global trade through the reduction of tariffs and other trade barriers. At first sight, it appears to be a much more democratic body than the IMF or World Bank, with all member states having an equal vote in the biannual Ministerial Conference and the permanent General Council in Geneva. Decisions require unanimity. In practice, however, the interests of the big trading nations dominate proceedings. They can afford much bigger delegations at the Ministerial Conferences and more thorough research on negotiating positions than the poorer countries. And most decisions take place in informal 'green room' meetings which are by invitation of the Director General only, and take place in secret. The results are then presented to the main Conference on a 'take it or leave it' basis. Developing countries can only then resist the outcome by threatening to end the proceedings altogether, as they did at Cancun in January 2004.

What I have called a minimalist agenda for democratising these institutions takes its starting-point from the premise that states remain the prime vehicle for protecting and promoting their citizens' interests at the international level; and it is through their state representatives that citizens should expect to exert whatever influence they can on these institutions. Democratisation requires us to consider arrangements at two different levels, therefore: how fairly power is distributed between state representatives within the international institutions themselves, and how effectively influence can be brought to bear upon state representatives through democratic processes at the national level. We could consider these under the democratic themes of representation, accountability, transparency and the rule of law respectively.

representation

The governing arrangements of the four international institutions outlined in the box above constitute a typical oligarchy, to use a term developed in chapter 1: the rule of the few over the many. In this case, the few comprise the already wealthy and powerful states of the developed world (excepting China's status in the UN Security Council). It is similar to the feudal system of the medieval era. This is simply indefensible on any consideration of equity, let alone broader democratic grounds. Pointing out that these states could exercise an effective veto on constitutional change does not make the situation any more defensible. Nor does the argument that in the IMF and World Bank these states contribute most of the capital, and so are justified in their privileged position. Not only is it profitable business for them, but by the end of the day the debtor countries will have paid back the capital a number of times over. Arguably, they have a stronger interest in the policies pursued by these organisations, since it is their economies that are most seriously affected by them.

The simplest reform proposal is to make the position of all states constitutionally equal in these institutions. In the case of the WTO, this would mean abolishing decision making by informal cabal, and establishing research facilities and resources that could be accessed by developing countries. In the case of the UN, merely adding some more permanent members to the Security Council, as is often advocated, would not produce equity. If it is contended that 'treating unequals equally', to use Aristotle's phrase, is unjust, because not all states carry equal weight, then votes and positions in the organisation should be allocated according to size of population, not wealth or military power. This would be the most democratic arrangement, and most in conformity with the principle that a country's delegate represents the interests of the country's people, not of the state itself. Voting arrangements in the Council of Ministers of the European Union operate according to this principle, so it is neither novel nor utopian. Resistance to it would seem to rely on the familiar, though unjustifiable, assumption that Western lives and interests count for more than non-Western ones.

accountability

According to this 'minimalist' model for the democratisation of international institutions, it should build on the familiar democratic procedures of the national level, and the prime mechanism for accountability should be by each country's representative to their own democratic institutions, not just to their government. Democratisation, therefore, should involve strengthening the scrutiny procedures of national legislatures and their specialist committees over their international representatives.

The objection that a country's foreign policies have never been subject to as much democratic accountability as its domestic ones cannot be an argument for perpetuating the situation, in a world where what happens beyond the country's borders is assuming so much importance. There are now significant 'attentive publics' and non-governmental organisations at the national level which have an intense interest in international affairs. These could be given a role in the process of domestic legislative scrutiny of the proceedings of international organisations, through consultative and observer status. Such an arrangement would help to counterbalance the existing situation whereby a country's representatives on international organisations speak for only limited domestic constituencies – for the financial community on the IMF, for particular business interests on the WTO, and so on. Accountability at the international level, in short, depends on the effectiveness of processes of accountability at the national level; the one determines the other.

transparency

Accountability depends on those to whom account is owed being fully informed. The simplest way to meet this requirement is for a full record of all meetings and proceedings of international organisations to be available on the Web, as well as other relevant

documentation. Although the WTO, for instance, has one of the
most extensive disclosure policies among international organisations, this does not apply to the key informal meetings in which
trade policy is actually determined, and whose content is therefore
not known even by all state members. The logic of accountability to
national legislatures would also suggest giving the members of their
specialist scrutiny committees observer status at the most important
international meetings.

the rule of law

A major defect of proposals for strengthening the accountability of
international bodies through national democratic procedures is that
not all countries are themselves democratic. This raises once more
the issue of whether democratisation can be facilitated from outside,
and whether the UN and its various bodies can have any role in this,
beyond support for the conduct of free elections once these have
been decided upon. To be sure, if the reforms of representation mentioned already were implemented, it would remove the impression
that any intervention was prompted by Western interests. Yet can the
UN have any role at all?

As we have seen, democratisation at country level depends primarily on the citizens of the country concerned, and the various
pressures they are able to bring upon their own government.
Influence from outside, other than through reinforcing a climate of
democratic norms at the international level, is difficult. In particular, most countries at the UN are deeply sensitive about having the
spotlight turned on their own imperfections, and are reluctant to do
so to others. As of yet, the UN is not an organisation of democratic
states, like the European Union, and so cannot make membership
dependent on a test of democratic credentials.

It may be that the most effective step in this direction would be
through a strengthening of the international human rights regime
which is already well established at UN level. All state signatories to
the civil and political rights covenant are required to produce five-
yearly reports on the state of human rights in their country to the
UN human rights committee, which has a quasi-judicial status. A
natural evolution would be for the committee to be turned into a
fully-fledged international court, with eventually the right of appeal
for citizens against their governments in case of the most serious
rights violations. As the experience of the European Court of

Human Rights has shown, judicial processes are often more acceptable means for effecting internal change from outside because of
their impartiality, than is pressure from other states. It may well be
that the best protection and promotion of a country's democracy
that can be achieved at the international level lies in a judicial mechanism for protecting the individual civil and political rights of its
citizens. At a later stage, this same process of jurisdiction could be
extended to include the activities of transnational corporations, as
well as governments.

towards a cosmopolitan democracy

It is an indication of how far we are away from democracy at the
international level that even the 'minimalist' programme outlined
above seems radical, even utopian. Yet those who advocate a more
far-reaching democratisation of international institutions take their
starting-point from the limitations of this agenda. Not that they
reject the idea of redressing the bias towards Western interests in
these institutions. What they take issue with is their state-centred
character, and the assumption that the only way people's interests
can be represented internationally is through their national governments, rather than more directly. Their proposals therefore focus on
a number of different ways in which the concerns of the world's
peoples might be articulated directly at the international level,
whether as a complement or an alternative to representation
through governments. The idea of 'cosmopolitan democracy'
proposes a regime of global governance in which people can engage
directly, as citizens of the world, rather than only as citizens of a
particular country.

> Democracy for the new millennium must involve cosmopolitan
> citizens able to gain access to, and mediate between, and render
> accountable, the social, economic and political processes and flows
> which cut across and transform their traditional community
> boundaries. The notion of cosmopolitan democracy recognizes our
> complex, interconnected world. It recognizes, of course, certain
> problems and policies as appropriate for local governments and
> national states; but it also recognizes others as appropriate for
> specific regions, and still others – such as environment, global security
> concerns, world health questions and economic regulation – that
> need new institutions to address them. (David Held, in Holden, ed.)

How might this cosmopolitan ideal be realised in practice? Some writers put their emphasis on the associations and networks of a global 'civil society', others on a directly elected global assembly or world parliament. Yet others see these arrangements as complementary, or propose additional mechanisms of popular engagement.

global civil society

We have already encountered the idea of civil society and its associational activity in chapter 2, as a key component of democracy at the national level. One starting-point for the idea of a global civil society is the observation that many voluntary associations already straddle the boundary between the national and the international arenas. Organisations such as Amnesty International, Oxfam, Save the Children, Greenpeace, and so on, already have a global reach and mission. Although older international federations, such as those of trade unions or women's institutes, may be in decline, their place has been taken by more recent social movements mobilised around women's issues, the environment, anti-capitalism, and so on. There are associations of indigenous peoples, endangered language groups and other minorities, which cut across national borders. Then there are transnational networks developed to campaign for specific policy changes on issues, such as HIV drugs, debt relief, or the banning of land mines. Or these may take a more permanent form, such as the World Social Forum, which meets on a regular basis.

The idea of a global citizenship is already prefigured in these non-governmental organisations, or NGOs. Many of them are already recognised by UN bodies in an ad hoc way. For example, the UN World Conference on Human Rights in Vienna in 1993 was attended by hundreds of NGOs, and similar numbers took part in the Conference on World Social Development in Copenhagen in 1995 and the World Conference on Women in Beijing the same year, in parallel with official state delegations. Human rights organisations have exercised a continuing influence on standard setting in international human rights instruments, such as the conventions on torture and on children's rights. After the anti-capitalist demonstrations at the G8 summit in Genoa in 2001, the IMF and World Bank responded to an invitation by a group of NGOs to engage in a dialogue about their policies, and the WTO has been involved in similar exercises. It would not be far-fetched to imagine such arrangements becoming routinised, and for coalitions of NGOs being given a permanent consultative status on these and other international organisations, where they could provide an alternative perspective to that of official state representatives. 'Globalisation from below' is one description of this process.

In playing this role, international NGOs have two advantages. Collectively, they can give voice to concerns which may be marginalised or even suppressed at the level of national government. And since they mostly specialise in individual issue areas, they are particularly suited to operating in an environment of international organisations which are themselves highly specialised.

> What we are seeing within the emerging framework of global governance is the parcellization of authority not on a territorial basis but on the basis of issues. We talk about a humanitarian regime, or a global climate change regime, or about global financial regulation … Governments appoint representatives to take decisions on these different issue areas and these are legitimate since they are appointed by elected governments. What participation of global civil society does is to provide an alternative vehicle for deliberation, for introducing normative concerns, for raising the interests of the individual and not just the state. (Mary Kaldor)

It is often objected that NGOs consist of self-appointed activists, who are unrepresentative of wider society, and may not be organised very democratically themselves. Yet their legitimacy can never be a formal representative one, which belongs to governments and parliaments by virtue of the electoral process. Their legitimacy comes from the importance and popular resonance of the viewpoints they articulate, the credibility of the arguments and evidence used to support them, and the opportunity for voluntary participation which they provide to ordinary citizens. It is for these reasons that they have already come to be taken seriously by international organisations.

world parliament

Proposals for the establishment of a World Parliament or Peoples' Assembly at the UN date back a long way. Such an assembly could be elected directly by the citizens of the world. Given the size of the constituencies needed to create a manageable assembly of six hundred or so (around ten million constituents) those elected would most likely be nationally known figures without any party affiliation. Such an assembly could have a dual role: deliberation on transnational issues, and scrutiny of the work of the multifarious UN agencies. Even if electoral turnouts were low, such an assembly would have enormous authority to speak on behalf of the world's peoples.

An elected assembly would complement, not replace, other UN organs. It would complement the existing General Assembly by introducing the representation of people, where the General Assembly represents states. And it would complement the contribution of NGOs, which, as we have seen, are single-issue bodies whose consultative role would be most usefully situated within the specialist UN agencies. Its supranational, rather than intergovernmental, status would be reinforced if it were financed not by contributions from national governments but by taxes levied directly on, say, international financial transactions or airline fuel, both of which would be economically or environmentally progressive.

> Let us picture a situation, for example, in which a body such as the World Bank had decided to pay for the construction of a giant hydro-electric dam. The villagers whose homes were due to be flooded might approach the world parliament and ask it to examine the bank's decision. The parliament would ask the bank for its comments, and perhaps send a fact-finding mission to the site of the dam. It would then judge the scheme by the principles it had established [for the bank's programmes]. If it found that the dam fell short of those principles, it would say so ... I think we can expect the bank to consider itself obliged to respond to the world parliament's decisions. (George Monbiot)

municipalities

A further set of candidates for participating in global governance on behalf of people are the world's municipalities, which share common problems across national borders, and offer greater opportunities for public participation in their solution than do national states. As the former UN Secretary General, Boutros Boutros-Ghali points out, these are already involved in the work of UN Commissions on Sustainable Development and Climate Change, and in disseminating good practice on participatory development processes at the local level.

> Already, the city is where global problems converge and where their interconnections are most apparent ... The city may also be the place where a sound basis for solving these problems can be built, for of all human settlements, cities are best placed to foster dialogue

and diversity, to engender community and a spirit of civic engagement while also opening windows to the world. Mayors and metropolitan authorities have therefore become indispensable agents for social integration within and among cities and thus within and among states. (Boutros Boutros-Ghali, in Holden, ed.)

In more polemical vein the peace activist Johann Galtung argues that local authorities are much better 'world citizens' than states. States possess armies, are expansionist and secretive, and their officials operate as a self-enclosed corps, especially in international organisations. Local authorities, by contrast, are peaceful and community-oriented, and already possess well-developed networks with authorities in other countries that bypass states and their power–political interests. They are therefore appropriate candidates for a more people-focused representation at the global level.

practical politics or pipedreams?

Most of these different proposals for a cosmopolitan democracy do not seek to replace existing institutions of governance at the international level, or the existing system of representation by governments. Their aim is to democratise them by involving popular constituencies and organisations which have a number of distinct advantages over representation through state delegates or ambassadors alone:

- They can articulate a range of popular concerns, whereas state delegates represent an official view, and that of the most powerful economic and political domestic interests.
- They are able to take a genuinely global view of problems, whereas state representatives are limited to considering and promoting primarily national interests.
- They offer the possibility of enhancing popular participation in global affairs, whereas state representatives tend to operate as self-enclosed élites.

This account may seem unduly optimistic, even romanticised. So it will be worth concluding this section by assessing these different proposals against the sceptical comment of Robert Dahl with which we began: the greater the size of the democratic unit, he argues, the more attenuated popular participation will be, and, by extension, the less influence people will have on the outcome.

The first set of proposals, which I have called a 'minimum agenda', does not fall quite so foul of this objection as the cosmopolitan ones. One part of this agenda, let us recall, involves a more equitable distribution of voting power between state representatives on the major international organisations, and is not affected by Dahl's objection. Another part involves enhancing existing democratic channels at national level for making state representatives on international bodies more domestically accountable. This again should meet Dahl's objection, because it keeps the scope of democratic accountability firmly within the orbit of national political processes, where he believes democracy properly belongs. Yet this level also seems very inadequate in face of the global issues which transcend national interests, and which the cosmopolitan alternative promises to address.

Yet is this more ambitious alternative realistic? If we think only of elections, then Dahl would seem to be correct. What meaningful contact could any one elector among ten million have with their international representative? However, there is a different way of looking at the matter. What many of the proposals stress is that more popular agencies of representation are able to articulate shared concerns of people which are not given sufficient weight by state representatives, who tend to be biased towards the most powerful domestic lobbies and interests: concerns about the environment, working conditions, women's issues, access to land and clean water, fair trade, and so on. The electoral process would give representatives greater authority to press these issues on the international agenda, even though the influence of any one elector may disappear to vanishing-point. The main purpose of an election, in other words, would be the collective *authorisation* and *legitimation* of representatives, rather than the value that could be assigned to any one individual's *participation*.

Even if we limit our focus to participation, however, Dahl seems too pessimistic. We only have to point to the effects of the international campaigns on land mines, debt relief, HIV drugs, and so on, which have only achieved what successes they have by mobilising large numbers of committed people across state borders. Huge numbers of people have attended anti-globalisation demonstrations, and continue to attend various alternative international forums. Civil society provides the most significant arena for active political participation in the contemporary world, whether at national or international levels. It does so because it enables people to forge a crucial link between participation and tangible policy outcome, which many no longer find in membership of political parties or electoral processes. The fact that it privileges the participation of those with the most *intense* views, who are thereby motivated to get off their backsides and do something about their concerns, is only a problem from a democratic perspective if those views are radically at variance with the majority of the less committed. And that is why they have to be set in the context of the formal process of electoral representation, where everyone's vote is equal.

Defenders of cosmopolitan democracy have one further point to make to its objectors. This is that democratisation is an evolving *process*, whose end-point is rarely clear and, even when clear, is never fully realised. There are setbacks and periods of crisis, which can serve as a springboard for further development, though often in a form that may not have been predicted. This characteristic of democracy as a process of coming-to-be is particularly true at the international level. The history of the evolution of the European Union has been precisely like this, and the final section of this chapter will briefly examine the EU as a transnational organisation which manifests in an exemplary way many of the democratic problems and possibilities we have just been considering.

democracy and the european union

The European Union (EU) is a highly complex organisation, but we do not have to tie ourselves in knots to make sense of it. A useful starting-point for understanding its institutions is to recognise that they are a combination of the *intergovernmental*, involving negotiations between national governments through their representatives, and the *supranational*, involving bodies whose remit is to consider the community interest as a whole, rather than particular national interests. This distinction is one we have already met in our discussion of international organisations in the previous section, and it is quite clearly demarcated in the case of the EU.

The intergovernmental aspect is represented by the *Council of Ministers*, which is the main law-making body of the EU. This is composed of departmental ministers and officials from all member states, with votes weighted according to the size of their respective populations. While decisions on many matters require unanimity, the practice of qualified majority voting (seventy per cent plus) has become increasingly common to avoid paralysis in decision making when changes are needed.

The supranational dimension is represented by three main institutions:

1. The *Commission*, whose task is to propose and prepare legislation for the Council of Ministers, as well as to supervise the implementation of the Union's laws and policies. Members of the Commission are appointed by national governments, approved by the European Parliament, and its president is the most important EU figure.
2. The *European Parliament (EP)*, which is directly elected by citizens of the member states according to the size of the country's population. Originally conceived as an advisory and debating chamber, it now has co-decision powers with the Council on some legislation, and scrutiny powers over the Commission, with the sanction of removing the whole Commission *en bloc*, as has happened already once.
3. The *European Court of Justice (ECJ)*, comprising fifteen judges appointed by member states, who adjudicate on matters of EU law. Among the most important decisions of the Court was one which established the primacy of EU law over national law. The ECJ should be distinguished from the European Court of Human Rights, which belongs to a different body (the Council of Europe) and is the final arbiter on violations of civil and political rights in member states.

To summarise this structure, the EU can best be described as a political organisation which combines intergovernmental and supranational elements, and operates on the basis of co-decision between its component institutions. But we should not also overlook the key role of member states, which have the responsibility for implementing and enforcing EU legislation in their own countries. People talk about the 'Brussels bureaucracy' as if it were some huge monster out of control. In fact it is very small, since most of the work of implementation and enforcement is carried out by member governments and their administrations. And these governments have separately to approve significant changes to the EU treaties through ratification by their own parliaments, and in some countries by popular referenda also.

is there a 'democratic deficit'?

To get a sense of how far the EU has already travelled in a democratic direction, it will be useful to compare its institutions with the UN bodies examined in the previous section. The following are some of the main differences:

- Citizens of EU member states have a common set of basic rights, which are enforceable by courts at the European level.
- The ECJ has the power to adjudicate and enforce EU law across all member states.
- There is a directly elected parliament, which has powers of co-decision with other EU institutions.
- In the Council of Ministers, countries have voting power proportionate to their populations.
- In most countries, the citizens have had the final right of decision on joining the EU, and in many of them approval of changes to EU treaties is by popular referendum.
- Access to EU membership is a powerful lever for the internal democratisation of applicant countries, since 'only democracies need apply'.

Most of these features – guaranteed individual rights, the enforceable rule of law, a directly elected assembly, the voting of state representatives weighted according to population, popular referenda, effective leverage for democratisation at country level – are precisely those which the proponents of democratisation at the international level have found wanting in the UN, as we have seen in the previous section. Yet there remains a widespread conviction among the peoples of Europe that the decision makers in Brussels who affect their lives are remote and unaccountable. And this conviction is reflected in an equally widespread view among expert commentators on the EU that there is a chronic 'democratic deficit' in its governing arrangements. As the saying goes, if the EU were ever required to apply for entry to its own organisation, it would be refused admission!

Where precisely this deficit in democracy lies, however, is a matter of considerable disagreement among these commentators. Depending on what sort of animal they think the EU is, they come up with very different criteria for judging its democratic credentials: as a quasi-state, as an intergovernmental organisation, or as some combination of the two.

the EU as a quasi-state

Those who see the EU as having pretensions to becoming a federal state are likely to assess its level of democracy by the criteria normally applied to the existing states we know. According to these criteria, the EU is seriously deficient in two key democratic aspects. First, there is no single decision-making centre which can be held responsible for any policy outcomes, since decision making is shared between different institutions. A key element in a democracy is the ability to 'throw the rascals out'. But in the EU, it is not clear who the 'rascals' are, nor, even if they could be identified, that the electorate could do anything about it.

Second, there is no European 'demos', or people with a common sense of identity, who could form the democratic subject of political action and engagement. People's primary political loyalties are to the national state. There is no common European language, no shared media of communication and no common public sphere in which the people can engage in debate about European issues. It is hardly surprising, therefore, that the public is so apathetic and poorly informed about EU affairs. It simply does not have the capacity to play any meaningful part in the Union, except when a purely national referendum shakes the system by its failure to endorse a new treaty, or when resistance to immigration from the new member states demonstrates how deeply entrenched are national identities, and how remote is the idea of a common European 'demos'.

the EU as an intergovernmental organisation

Those who see the EU primarily as an intergovernmental organisation will identify its democratic deficit in the lack of effective national control over its collective decision making. From this point of view, the key drawback of the EU is the practice of qualified majority voting in the Council of Ministers, whereby a country's representative can be outvoted on an important issue, and so cannot be held accountable for it back home, where accountability properly belongs. How can a representative be held accountable for a decision he or she did not take? From this perspective, the deficit lies primarily in the fact that the EU has moved away from being a strictly intergovernmental arrangement. The weakness of national democratic control is further contributed to by the secrecy with which proceedings in the Council of Ministers are conducted, and the inadequacy of effective parliamentary oversight of ministers and officials acting in an EU capacity.

the EU as a mixed form of governance

A third view argues that, since the EU is neither a simple intergovernmental organisation nor a state, neither of the first two criteria for assessing its democratic condition are appropriate. We need criteria which recognise its distinctive character as a mix of intergovernmental and supranational bodies, working together. From this perspective, we can see: strong public accountability, in the way the different institutions act as a check on each other; strong representation of citizens through the combination of the Parliament and national representatives in the Council of Ministers; strong defence of basic rights through the combination of adjudication at national and European levels, and so on. The first two perspectives simply fail to grasp the EU's distinctive character, and their judgements therefore underestimate its democratic qualities.

Even from this more optimistic perspective, however, the big gap in public engagement and interest has to be counted a negative feature. Whatever criterion of democracy may be employed, you cannot have democracy if the people themselves are largely absent. Yet there are some arguments for suggesting that the situation here is not as serious as at first sight it appears:

- Much EU policy concerns technical economic and trading issues. The areas of government which most citizens get worked up about – health, education, social security, pensions, law and order, taxation – remain the preserve of national states and their democratic processes.
- The fact that we have not seen any public mobilisations directed at EU policy to compare with the massive global demonstrations against the war in Iraq or the international financial institutions, or the campaigns against land mines or global debt, may be because the EU Parliament acts as an effective vehicle for transmitting citizens' concerns, even though few bother to vote.
- Institutions can be created or changed quickly, whereas loyalties and identities take much longer to develop; so it is still early days for the development of a common European 'demos' alongside existing national identities. In any case, it may be at the social level, through music, travel, sport and use of a common currency, that such identities evolve, rather than through political institutions as such.

There is something to be said for each of these arguments. Yet an engaged public opinion is an important resource for any democratic institution. And the failure to identify any means for engaging the public more systematically in the Union, such as Europe-wide elections to choose the president of the Commission, must be regarded as a significant defect in the EU's new constitution.

conclusion

We started with a problem: so much that affects the welfare of a country's citizens now has its source outside the state's borders and lies beyond the government's control. Yet this national level is the one where our familiar institutions of representative democracy have their origin and their continuing location. Can democracy in any meaningful sense be realised beyond this level, in the international institutions which promise some control over these cross-border and global forces?

We have seen that a completely sceptical answer to this question is implausible. Despite talk of its democratic deficit, the EU demonstrates that many of the proposals for democratisation of the UN, which are dismissed as utopian, have already been realised at this regional level. The EU's combination of intergovernmental and supranational arrangements provides an obvious model for the larger international sphere, with democratic representation and accountability operating in both dimensions. Active citizen participation and engagement still remains problematic. Yet the relative success of a number of citizen-driven campaigns and mobilisations across borders at the global level suggests the potential for engagement is there.

It may be that regional organisations constitute a necessary stage on the way to a more effective and democratic international order. To be sure, Europe has had some distinctive advantages in this regard. The member countries of the EU were already democratic, and enjoyed a shared cultural heritage and developed economies. In this respect, Europe is more homogeneous than many other regions of the world. Yet we should not forget the EU's origin in the devastating conflicts of two world wars, to which must now be added the transcendence of the post-1945 division of the continent by the Cold War. In sum, there is as much ground for optimism as for pessimism about international democracy. As with democracy anywhere, it ultimately depends on the determination of the people themselves.

further reading

Archibugi, Daniele, David Held and Martin Koehler, eds. *Re-imagining Political Community: Studies in Cosmopolitan Democracy*. Cambridge: Polity Press, 1998.

Fisher, William and Thomas Ponniah, eds. *Another World is Possible*. London and New York: Zed Books, 2003.

Held, David. *Global Covenant*. Cambridge: Polity Press, 2004.

Holden, Barry. ed. *Global Democracy: Key Debates*. London and New York: Routledge, 2000.

Kaldor, Mary. *Global Civil Society*. Cambridge: Polity Press, 2003.

Lord, Christopher. *Democracy in the European Union*. Sheffield: Sheffield Academic Press, 1998.

Monbiot, George. *The Age of Consent*. London: Flamingo, 2003.

Shapiro Ian, and Casiano Hacker-Cordon, eds. *Democracy's Edges*. Cambridge: Cambridge University Press, 1999.

Siedentop, Larry. *Democracy in Europe*. London and New York: Penguin Press, 2000.

Singer, Peter. *One World*. New Haven and London: Yale University Press, 2002.

reviving democracy: new forms of participation

One conclusion that can be drawn from the previous chapter is that, whatever developments in democratisation may be possible at the international level, the main site for democracy and popular involvement will remain at the different levels of government within national states. Yet, as we have also seen from previous chapters, there is widespread disaffection among the public in both new and old democracies about the way their governments operate, and in their own capacity to influence them. How can this disaffection be reduced? In this chapter, we shall examine a number of initiatives that have been developed to involve people more directly in their own self-government, not as an alternative to representative democracy, but as a necessary complement and corrective to it.

Some of these initiatives are very local; some are national. Some of them have been around a long time; some are very recent and innovative. What they all share is the attempt to give citizens more control over their collective affairs, and in ways that they experience as empowering. All of them build on resources that are already available within civil society, which, as we have seen in chapter 2, is a key site for the self-organisation of citizens in any democracy. Yet they seek to find ways of extending these resources, and linking them more systematically with the work of government.

Four different modes of direct participation by citizens will be examined and assessed:

1. Co-decision in devolved government.
2. Deliberative polls and citizens' juries.
3. Referenda and citizens' initiatives.
4. Digital Democracy.

This list is selective rather than exhaustive. It contains quite diverse forms of participation. Yet all offer ways of reinvigorating the practice of representative democracy and the relation between people and government through a more involved citizenry. Before examining them in turn, I shall introduce some more general issues about the practice of participatory democracy.

participation in government

The idea of participatory democracy – of people taking part in person in the running of their own government – has been around ever since the citizen assemblies of ancient Athens. Even with the development of representative democracy in the modern world the idea has never completely gone away. Town meetings in the East Coast of the USA, citizen assemblies in the Swiss cantons, parish meetings in rural England – these are rare survivors of a less populous age. Much more dramatic have been the mass mobilisations in revolutionary periods, which have not only overthrown oppressive regimes but have also spawned a host of spontaneous forms of popular organisation for managing collective affairs – everything from food distribution to citizen defence and the control of crime. What these revolutionary periods have demonstrated is the enormous reservoir of untapped capacities in ordinary people, and that the collapse of normal government does not necessarily result in chaos or disorganisation. Similar lessons can be drawn from many lesser emergencies, such as the women's organisations which sprang up during the 1984 miners' strike in Britain, to provide a host of communal facilities, as well as to campaign in their own right. 'The women have changed. They have discovered a strength, a talent, a voice, an identity, that they never knew existed,' said one participant. A key question for the proponents of participatory government is whether the activism of these exceptional periods can be reproduced in more normal times, and in the context of a representative democracy. Here is what the eighteenth-century English democrat Tom Paine, who took part in both the American and French revolutions, had to say:

> It appears to general observation, that revolutions create genius and talents; but those events do no more than bring them forward. There is existing in man [sic] a mass of sense lying in a dormant state, and which, unless something excites it to action, will descend with him, in that condition, to the grave. As it is to the advantage of society that the whole of its faculties should be employed, the construction of government ought to be such as to bring forward, by a quiet and regular operation, all that extent of capacity which never fails to appear in revolutions.

Or we might consider this from John Stuart Mill in the nineteenth century:

> The first question in respect to any political institutions is, how far they tend to foster in the members of the community the various desirable qualities, moral, intellectual and active. The government which does this best has every likelihood of being the best in all other respects, since it is on these qualities, so far as they exist in the people, that all possibility of goodness in the practical operations of the government depends.

These two quotations encapsulate many of the hopes that present-day proponents of participatory schemes invest in them. Their claims for the benefits of active participation could be summarised in the following points:

* Governmental arrangements which can harness the knowledge and capacities of ordinary people, and not just the 'experts', will produce better quality government, which is also more in touch with popular needs.
* Participation enhances people's own knowledge and competence as they address practical problems in their communities.
* The process of deliberating with others about solutions to such problems leads participants to modify their personal preferences in the light of evidence and the needs of others and to consider a wider public interest.
* Being able to see tangible outcomes from one's participation produces a sense of empowerment and an incentive to continue one's involvement.

- Government at large becomes more responsive and attuned to a wider range of needs than it otherwise would.

The proponents of participatory schemes, however, not to mention their critics, are also aware that there may be disadvantages or pitfalls in involving people more actively in government. Typical dilemmas include these:

- Involving more people in the work of government may simply reinforce existing inequalities, since the educated and well-off tend to be the ones with the skills and motivation to become involved.
- Popular forums are very vulnerable to capture by small groups whose agendas may be quite unrepresentative of the wider population.
- To ask ordinary citizens to contribute to decision making where complex questions needing technical expertise are decided may be asking too much of them.
- The parameters of decision making may be so constrained by external powers that the issues which really concern people may be simply 'off limits'.
- Participation in practice may be nothing more than 'pseudo-participation', where people are merely consulted and government is under no obligation to take any notice of the results.

How far these problems can be overcome in the different modes of participation to be considered will be an important test of their quality. Indeed, this list of benefits and pitfalls can provide a useful set of criteria to refer back to as we proceed.

co-decision in devolved government

The most basic point at which people experience the effects of government policy is at the most local level where they live. This is the level where problems directly impinge on them, relating to housing, water supply, sanitation, roads, access to public services, transport, crime and the environment generally – and where government failings are immediately evident. This is also the level where citizens are most able to meet with others in face-to-face contact, and where social networks may already be quite well-developed. This is the most obvious level, therefore, at which people can become directly involved in government.

In recent years, there have been in many countries numerous experiments with devolving local decision making to people themselves. Most of these have been restricted to specific sectors. For example, tenants of social housing have been given responsibility for determining priorities for improvement and repair of their properties; in some cases, the resources for management and improvement have been devolved completely to them. Neighbourhood residents have been given responsibility of co-decision with the local police about priorities and methods for dealing with crime in their neighbourhood. Parents and other residents have been given joint responsibility with teachers for the running of schools through elected schools councils, which report back regularly to meetings of their respective constituencies.

Most of these initiatives have not been prompted by a generalised desire for more participation *per se*. They have been a response to a widely perceived failure of existing governmental structures to solve pressing problems, and a recognition that they can only be solved with the active involvement of those most affected: by tenants taking care of their immediate environment, residents co-operating in preventative strategies against crime, and parents supporting improvements in their children's learning and school attendance. Yet their involvement could most effectively be secured and maintained only by devolving substantial responsibility to them, and building new participatory decisional structures through which this responsibility could be realised. One conclusion, then, is that extending grassroots participation is less likely to occur when things are going reasonably well. Another is that it depends on the existing government at some level recognising the need for it, and actively encouraging and supporting it, as well as pressure coming from people themselves.

Both these features are evident in much more ambitious and wide-ranging initiatives, covering multiple sectors, that have been attempted in recent years. Two examples will be outlined here, which have attracted much attention and commentary among academics and practitioners alike. One is the system of participatory budgeting in the city of Porto Alegre in southern Brazil. The other is the campaign for decentralised planning in the state of Kerala in South India. *(both ltd.)*

participatory budgeting in porto alegre

The city of Porto Alegre is now famous for its experiment, begun in 1989 when the Workers' Party (PT) took control of the city council, with devolving decisions about the spending of the municipal budget to citizens at local level. They meet in large assemblies in each of the sixteen districts of the city to determine public projects for their district, and investment priorities for the city as a whole. Each of the assemblies elects delegates to meet regularly in district and thematic meetings where projects are firmed up in collaboration with city officials. These are then brought back to the district assemblies for ratification, where two councillors for each district are elected to serve on the Municipal Council for the Budget, along with representatives of the five thematic committees. The Council has the task of agreeing an overall city budget, which is sent to the mayor for final approval. The numbers of people participating in the various meetings might look like this:

- District assemblies up to one thousand in each district, meeting twice in the budget cycle.
- District delegate meetings: around fifty each, meeting weekly during the early months.
- Municipal Council of the Budget: thirty-two district delegates, plus thematic and other representatives, meeting regularly during the later months of the budget process.

The origin of participatory budgeting lay in the desire to break with the old system of bureaucratic allocation of city resources on a patronage basis ('who knows and owes favours to whom'), which had become widely discredited. The new participatory system not only makes budgeting wholly transparent, but has succeeded in redistributing resources towards the poorer areas of the city, as well as increasing the overall tax collection rates. Among other distinctive features of the process are: the provision of training seminars in budgeting for delegates; the regular monitoring of past projects, which takes place at the first district assemblies of the budgeting cycle, and the regular review and improvement of the participatory process itself, which is the responsibility of the Municipal Council of the Budget.

decentralised planning in kerala

Kerala is one of the poorest states in India, but a succession of left-wing governments has ensured it one of the highest literacy rates in the federation. In 1996, the Communist-led Left Democratic Front inaugurated a People's Campaign for Decentralised Planning, under which some forty per cent of the state's budget was devolved from the state's powerful line departments to around nine hundred village planning councils. Under the scheme, each village was required to produce a development plan including assessments of local need, plans for specific projects and their beneficiaries, and details of financing and monitoring arrangements.

The starting-point of the planning process is the village assembly open to all citizens, which reviews areas of need, and elects delegates to prepare a development strategy and detailed project proposals. A series of training seminars is provided for the delegates, to prepare them for this work. Once plans are worked out and locally agreed, they are then submitted to local elected councils, and from there to higher councils for co-ordination at district level, and assessment for technical and fiscal viability. The overall state-wide numbers participating in the different stages of this process in the first year of the scheme in 1997–8 were as follows:

- Village assemblies: two million in total, meeting twice in the planning cycle.
- Development seminars for delegates: three hundred thousand.
- Task forces to prepare projects: one hundred thousand.
- Higher tier planning meetings: five thousand.

As at Porto Alegre, the decentralisation initiative in Kerala has succeeded in redistributing development resources to deprived areas and groups in a society marked by high levels of inequality, through mobilising grass-roots participation in defining priority needs, such as housing, drinking water and sanitation. In addition, given the high levels of corruption throughout India (see box on p. 87), the greater transparency has helped erode the traditional relationship between contractors, engineers and politicians in decisions about development projects. Other distinctive features have been the strong involvement of elected councillors in the process, and the mobilisation of thousands of voluntary experts, many retired, to give technical advice and evaluation to the projects submitted from the grass roots.

overall assessment

How should we evaluate these schemes in relation to the criteria for participation, and its potential pitfalls, outlined earlier (p. 132)? Both schemes have involved impressive numbers of participants, and on a repeated basis, which indicates that the tangible project outcomes have provided sufficient incentive for people to stay involved. Inevitably it has proved more difficult to achieve a high quality of deliberation in large assemblies, though in Kerala the practice has been introduced of breaking into small group discussion with facilitators. In addition, informal discussions have continued with delegates at neighbourhood and village level throughout the process. In both schemes, the participants at the lowest level have been quite representative of their respective populations, though at higher levels a bias towards males and the better educated has been evident. In both schemes also, the provision of extensive training programmes has served to enhance people's capacities.

Compared with participatory local schemes elsewhere, the agendas have not been so predetermined at the outset that people have been unable to achieve meaningful ownership of the process, since the role of government has been deliberately facilitative rather than prescriptive. This can be compared, for instance, with the experience of 'community led' schemes of urban regeneration in the UK, under the Labour Government's New Deal for Communities. In these, the pressure from central government on the Development Boards to achieve pre-set targets, together with the involvement of non-elected public bodies, with their own rules and agendas, has considerably diluted the quality of participation by local residents.

How far, finally, are the schemes in Porto Alegre and Kerala replicable elsewhere? Both have been the product of enlightened governing parties and specific circumstances in the communities themselves. Yet their success shows what can be achieved by people themselves at the most local level in tandem with a progressive government, and they offer an eminently realisable model for other places.

deliberative polls and citizens' juries

When systematic opinion polling was first introduced by George Gallup in the USA in the 1930s, his hope was that his method of sampling a cross-section of the population would be able to reproduce the effects of a New England town meeting on a national stage. Having read the newspapers and heard radio discussions on the issues of the day, the people sampled would be able to provide an accurate reflection of what the nation as a whole thought about the issue, even though they had never debated it face to face. Unfortunately, Gallup's conclusion proved unduly optimistic. Certainly, his sampling methods produced an accurate reflection of the state of public opinion. But most of the public had never read or heard the debates, and had not even thought about the questions they might be asked by a pollster to decide on. Their opinions were merely knee-jerk reactions. (NP-65)

Worse than that. Subsequent research showed that, when asked to comment on entirely fictitious events or personalities, respondents expressed just as confident an opinion as they did on the real ones. In one experiment on US attitudes to different types of immigrant, the greatest hostility was shown to the Wallonians and Pireneans, both non-existent groups. It is hardly surprising that politicians should be reluctant to bend to the views expressed in opinion polls; they, after all, are the ones supposedly best placed to give a properly reflective judgement, based on debate and evidence. Indeed, this is the argument that has always been advanced for leaving decisions firmly in the hands of our representatives.

It is to meet this objection that the idea of deliberative opinion polls has been developed, through the work of James Fishkin and various centres in the USA and elsewhere. The idea is to assemble a representative sample of the population in one place for several days, perhaps over a long weekend, so as to deliberate on a pressing question of the moment in small groups and plenaries. The activity of deliberation involves two components: one is exposure to, and questioning of, expert witnesses on the issue at stake; the other is participating in debate with those holding opposing arguments and opinions, and trying to arrive at a common view. The unreflective opinions with which people began the process could be expected to be modified in two corresponding ways: they would become more informed by accurate evidence; they would also take account of the opinions and arguments of others, even though they did not fully agree with them. The outcome of such a process would carry much greater authority than an ordinary opinion poll, as the reflective judgement of the nation, of the 'ideal public' as it were. It could have even more political impact if the proceedings and conclusions were also televised.

An ordinary poll models what the electorate thinks, given how little it knows. A deliberative opinion poll models what the electorate would think if, hypothetically, it could be immersed in intensive deliberative processes. The point of a deliberative opinion poll is prescriptive, not predictive. It has recommending force, telling us that this is what the entire mass public would think about some policy issues or some candidates if it could be given an opportunity for extensive reflection and access to information. (James Fishkin)

But isn't such deliberation just what we elect our representatives to do on our behalf? Do they not constitute just such a microcosm of the population as a whole? There are two problems here. First, they are not at all representative. Not only do they comprise a special caste of politicos, mostly male, who occupy a largely self-enclosed hothouse environment; they are also drawn disproportionately from wealthy, professional backgrounds. In the second place, they are subject to all kinds of pressures from special interests, to whom they may owe obligations, so that the process of decision they engage in is far removed from the deliberative ideal of classical representative theory.

The deliberative opinion poll comes much closer to that deliberative ideal, in which inequalities of power are not involved, beyond those intrinsic to the process of debate itself. The poll also embodies a key selection device, which Athenian democracy regarded as the most democratic possible: selection by lot. In a lottery, everyone has an equal chance to be selected; and, over time, with the rotation of tasks such as jury service, everyone may eventually be so. The lottery is the ultimate expression of political equality: one person is equally interchangeable with another, without regard for the circumstances.

According to Fishkin, the deliberative opinion poll thus manages to square the circle of two competing democratic imperatives. On the one hand is the requirement of deliberation; on the other that of political equality. Procedures or institutions designed to meet the first of these, such as the deliberations of an elected assembly, cannot meet the second. On the other hand, procedures which embody the principle of political equality, such as opinion polls or referenda, fail entirely on the deliberative dimension. The great merit of the deliberative opinion poll is that it combines the two, and does so uniquely.

Deliberative opinion polls are not, however, intended to *replace* the system of representative democracy, but to complement it. Fishkin himself originally envisaged introducing such a poll as a component in US primary elections for presidential candidates. A representative sample of six hundred electors would discuss the issues with the candidates over a three-day period, and would then arrive at their preferences after their own deliberation. The results would be widely publicised. Something similar took place in the *Granada 500* experiments in the UK during the 1970s and 1980s, in which a random sample of electors from a marginal constituency debated with experts about the parties' programmes for government, and then travelled to London to question party leaders live on national television.

citizens' juries

Citizens' juries operate with a very similar procedure to deliberative opinion polls, and are animated by a similar belief that ordinary citizens are perfectly capable of taking reflective decisions on complex issues, if given time to weigh the evidence and arguments. Typically, such juries are used to advise government at local or national level on a complex or controversial policy question, and to stimulate public debate about it. In this, they are very different from the focus groups of swing voters, beloved of governments, which are not representative of the wider population and operate entirely in secret. Citizens' juries were initially developed in the 1980s in parallel by the Jefferson Centre in Minneapolis, USA, and at the University of Wuppertal in Germany. Their use has since become widespread, though sometimes under different names, such as the 'consensus conferences' of Denmark and Holland.

> A consensus conference is a forum in which a group of lay people put questions about a scientific or technological subject of controversial political and social interest to experts, listen to the experts' answers, then reach a consensus about this subject and finally report their findings at a press conference. (Simon Joss and John Durant, Science Museum Library, London)

What sorts of issues have been considered by these juries? Here is a selection: urban design and physical planning; the choice of technologies for energy production and waste disposal; welfare reform; GM crops; priorities for medical treatment, and taxation policy. It may well happen that, when a jury is presented with a question to decide, such as which is the best route for a new motorway, they come up with another, such as should it be built at all? A citizens' jury in Cologne, invited to decide between different

AMERICA'S TOUGH CHOICES: THE 1993 FEDERAL BUDGET

In the citizens' jury on the US Federal budget, the first two days were spent presenting jurors with three points of view: the proposals made by President Clinton; a conservative point of view; and an alternative liberal view. Each of these was backed up by written material on six major spending areas of the Federal budget and on revenues and deficits. The jury then split into smaller discussion groups. On days three and four, three sets of eight jurors broke into expenditure groups to come up with specific recommendations regarding government spending in specific areas. On the afternoon of day four and in the first hour of day five, the whole jury reviewed the findings of the spending committees.

When jurors began their deliberations, about fifty per cent said they favoured cutting taxes and only seventeen per cent were in favour of raising them. During the course of the project, many changed their attitude. The citizens' jury proposed raising taxes by $70 billion: on alcohol and tobacco ($20 billion), on income tax on incomes over $200,000 ($30 billion) and on energy ($20 billion). They decided that defence spending should be cut more than the President planned, and that social security should be cut by $9 billion, compared with Clinton's proposals for a $6 billion cut, primarily by pruning administrative costs. Other proposals included raising the retirement age, taxing benefits of higher income citizens, and decreasing the budget for physical infrastructure by $15 billion, compared with Clinton's increase of $24 billion.

architectural designs for a new town hall, decided that more important was the preservation of open space in front of it, which did not figure in any of the plans. And if one wants further proof of the difference between the views of ordinary citizens and their elected representatives, then here is an example from a citizens' jury on health reform in the USA: in favour of comprehensive healthcare coverage, unanimous; in favour of members of the government, Congress and the judiciary living under whatever healthcare plan they introduced for the rest of the country, also unanimous.

overall assessment

In conclusion, we should ask how this method of participation measures up against the criteria outlined on p. 132, including the pitfalls to be avoided. Strong points include an almost ideal deliberative context and process, which is capable of addressing complex issues. It enables government policy to be more responsive by harnessing the reflective views of a cross-section of ordinary voters. The way the jury is selected prevents any bias towards the well-to-do or the politically active; and for those who take part, the experience can be a transformative one.

These are considerable advantages. On the downside is the obvious fact that the numbers involved constitute a drop in the ocean of the public at large, and a fraction of the numbers engaged in the devolved government initiatives described in the previous section. Of course, this is the whole point of a sample survey, that powerful conclusions can be drawn from the involvement of so few. But that means that only a few can also benefit from the experience. A second disadvantage is that elected governments are not bound to take any notice of the conclusions of a citizens' jury. So the sense of empowerment which comes from making a difference to policy outcomes, rather than just to their own life experience, is correspondingly reduced. Even then, it is a one-off event, and not a repeated one, as in the first mode of participation already analysed. Despite these limitations, however, the evidence is that governments at all levels are increasingly using citizens' juries to assess informed public opinion on controversial political questions.

referenda and citizens' initiatives

A referendum is a direct vote by the electorate on a legislative or constitutional proposal, inviting a straight 'yes' or 'no' response. In most democracies, all constitutional amendments have to be approved in this way by the people, and the results of a referendum are binding on the government. The rationale for direct citizen involvement here in a representative system is that the constitution belongs to the people, not to the legislature or government of the day. As the ultimate source of political authority, only the people can approve a constitution in the first place, and only they have the right to decide on any changes to it.

In some countries, such as the UK, which has no written constitution, a decision to hold a referendum is a matter for the government of the day. In 1975, the Labour Cabinet was so internally divided over whether the UK should remain a member of the European Economic Community that it decided to appeal to the people to resolve the issue, and members of the government campaigned on both sides. Since then, there have been referenda on: devolved government in Scotland, Wales, Northern Ireland and London; for the introduction of mayors in some English cities; referenda are promised on regional government in England, on electoral reform nationwide, and on the EU constitution and joining the common European currency zone. Although the UK's basic constitutional principle has always been that sovereignty resides in *parliament* and not in the *people*, it is now very difficult for a government to resist demands for an appeal to the people on major constitutional questions, especially where public opinion is sharply divided.

Could referenda not be used more widely, for normal legislative proposals as well as for constitutional amendments? Two countries have a long history of doing so, and offer a practical example of how citizens might be involved directly in the work of legislation. These are Switzerland and the USA. In the latter, the possibility exists only at state or city level, while in Switzerland it exists on the level of federal legislation. There are two main ways in which the citizens may act directly, over and above the obligatory requirement for a referendum on constitutional change which has already been discussed:

1. *The optional referendum on legislation.* Here, citizens may demand a referendum on any laws being considered by the legislature, if they can obtain the required number of valid signatures to do so. A referendum of all electors is then held within a given period. This provision effectively gives citizens a *negative* or *veto* power over legislation.
2. *The constitutional initiative.* As the term implies, this gives citizens a *positive* right of initiating a referendum on their own proposals for legislation, again subject to obtaining the required number of signatures. Although these technically count as constitutional amendments, their subject-matter is often that of normal legislation, and the boundary between a constitutional and a normal legislative provision becomes quite blurred as a result.

Although the provisions for both types of referendum are similar in Switzerland and the twenty-four US states which provide for them, their historical origin is quite different. Switzerland has had a long tradition of direct democracy, reaching back to the thirteenth century, when some of the cantons developed the institution of the annual meeting of all citizens to approve legislation. The referendum was the natural extension of this practice, once populations became too large to meet together in one place. In the USA, the institution of popular referenda and initiatives was a product of the Progressive Movement (1890–1920), which sought a counterweight to the corruption of state governments and the boss control of city politics, by giving a direct power to the people. The innovation appealed particularly to the Western states of the Union, where the Movement was strongest. It will be worth giving a brief summary of how these devices of direct democracy have been used in the two countries, before giving an assessment of their value and wider applicability.

switzerland

Before the 1970s, the right of positive constitutional initiative was very rarely used in Switzerland, compared with the right to call a referendum in opposition to a proposed law of the federal assembly. Since then, initiatives have become much more frequent, partly as a result of the growth of social movements and protest campaigns, especially on environmental and consumer issues; partly also because of the rise of professional 'initiative entrepreneurs', able to organise the collection of signatures across the country. In the twenty years between 1974 and 1993, the Swiss voted in no fewer than 167 referenda (an average of eight per year), of which sixty-three were positive initiatives proposed by citizen groups.

In terms of success, however, only four of these initiatives gained the required majority to pass, compared with seventy-seven of all other referenda in this period. At first sight, these figures give the impression that the people's veto power (saying 'no' to proposed parliamentary legislation) is much more effective than their positive power of initiative, and that they are averse to change. Yet there were other initiatives that were withdrawn before they ever got to a referendum, because they had been successfully used as a bargaining counter to extract favourable legislation or referendum proposals from the

Table 6.1 Subject-matter of Swiss initiatives submitted 1974–1993

Subject	Number
Environment, energy, traffic restrictions, animal rights	29
Consumer or renter protection, price controls	10
Defence, military policy	7
Antiforeigners	7
Taxes, economic policy	7
Workplace, employment	6
Social insurance	5
Women's issues, abortion	4
Agriculture	4
Alcohol, tobacco and drug abuse	3
Education	2
Others	6
Total	90

Source: David Butler and Austin Ranney, eds. *Referendums around the World*, p. 144.

government itself. So we could conclude that the positive power of initiative is a significant legislative force alongside the people's veto power, and that legislators have continually to look over their shoulders in anticipation of a possible referendum. It has been well said that legislation in Switzerland is the art of avoiding a referendum, and that direct democracy is the real parliamentary opposition.

Table 6.1 shows the subject-matter of all the initiatives submitted over the twenty-year period, that is, all those that passed the first stage of the initiative process, before proceeding either to a referendum or to withdrawal. The environmental and consumer issues are the most frequent, but it is worth noting the initiative of 1989 to abolish the army altogether, which received thirty-six per cent of the popular vote. No one can say that the agenda of possible initiatives is in any way constricted!

Referenda in Switzerland are not timed to coincide with the normal electoral cycle, as in the US, though they tend to be grouped together, so that on a typical referendum day electors will have more than one to vote on. For example, on 27 September 1992 the electors voted on the proposals overleaf with a fairly average turnout of forty-five per cent of the electorate:

- Construction of a trans-Alpine railway for automobiles (passed).
- Revised procedures for legislation (passed).
- Changes to banking tax (passed).
- Farmers' inheritance regulations (passed).
- Increase in MPs' salaries and funding for political parties (failed).
- Improved facilities and administrative services for MPs (failed).

the usa

Twenty-four states in the USA have constitutional provision for legislative initiative, as well as other types of referendum, and many major cities do likewise. In the states that have them, their success rate is about one in three. Table 6.2 gives a breakdown of the subject-matter of all initiatives in the states of the US during the period 1978 to 1992, for comparison with table 6.1 for Switzerland. Conservative activists tend to favour tax-cutting initiatives; liberals favour abortion rights and the freezing of nuclear power. A successful initiative in one state may spawn copycat proposals in others, such as the famous Proposition 13 in California in 1978, reducing and setting limits to property taxes. More recently, proposals to set term limits to state and Congressional representatives have enjoyed considerable

Table 6.2   Subject-matter of qualified initiatives in the US States, 1978–1992

Subject	Number
Revenue or tax or bond	105
Government or political reform	77
Regulation of business or labour	65
Public morality	58
Environment or land use	35
Civil liberties or rights	20
Health, welfare, housing	19
National policy	11
Education	9
Total	399

Source: *Referendums around the World*, p.238.

success. These reflect the same hostility to the representative process which led to the introduction of the popular initiative in the first place (and compare with the Swiss hostility to the improvement in MPs' pay and conditions).

Some commentators argue that the institution of the initiative has now been taken out of the hands of ordinary citizens and become simply another tool of the same dominant forces that shape the representative process in the US: the political parties and business finance. A recent example was the Republican-inspired initiative in California to recall the Democrat governor Gray Davis after only ten months in office, and replace him with Arnold Schwarzenegger. Yet an examination of all the initiatives passed in the state of California in the latest decade from 1991–2000 suggests more a populist than a business-oriented agenda, even though an average of two-thirds of initiative campaign funding is contributed by business (see table 6.3).

Does such a list vindicate the objections of those who say that the practice of direct democracy simply panders to the lowest prejudices of the electorate, and that one of the tasks of a representative system is to save the people from themselves? It should be pointed out here that there is an important line of defence against initiatives which are discriminatory or infringe minority rights, and that is with the courts, which have been very active in California in striking down referenda as unconstitutional where they infringe basic rights. A similar point could be made in answer to those who object to any direct democracy in the UK, on the grounds that the first item to be passed by popular vote would be the reintroduction of capital punishment. Since this is now outlawed under the European Convention of Human Rights as a 'cruel and unusual punishment', its reintroduction would similarly have to be ruled unconstitutional by UK courts. Provided there is a strong line of defence for basic rights, therefore, and equality before the law, one of the main objections to a referendum process loses its force.

Of more concern is the objection from supporters of the deliberative opinion poll, to the effect that there is no guarantee that voters will have listened to the public debate, or even that they will understand the terms of the propositions set before them. In the California election of 1990, for example, the ballot paper ran to 221 pages, so it was debatable whether the voters could even manage to read it, let alone understand the issues. This example is no doubt extreme. Yet there is an important argument on the other side. A referendum is

Table 6.3   Successful initiatives, California, 1991–2000

Year	Subject
1992	Public employee retirement systems
	End taxation of certain food products
	Term limits on Congressional representatives
1994	Mandatory life sentence for felons with two previous convictions
	Illegal aliens ineligible for public social services, health care or education
1996	Create open blanket primary voting
	Restrictions on campaign contributions and spending, and on lobbyists
	End to racial preferences
	Increase in minimum wage
	Regulations governing uninsured motorists and drunk drivers
	Legalise marijuana for medicinal purposes
	Establish tax limits
1998	State guidelines for early childhood and smoking prevention programmes
	Informed voter law
	End bilingual education
	End trapping mammals for fur
	Terms and conditions of compact for gambling on tribal land
	Outlaw possession or transfer of horses, ponies, etc. for killing
2000	Life sentences for violent crime; death penalty for gang-related murder
	Only marriages between man and woman valid
	Override restrictions on public contracting with private firms
	Mandatory drug treatment programme for certain drug offences
	Bonds authorised for school building and rehabilitation
	Total initiatives passed 1991–2000 — 23
	Total initiatives failed — 31

Source: Initiative and Referendum Institute, University of Southern California.

not the same as an opinion poll. In the latter, no responsibility is attached to the answer one gives. In a referendum, the voters know that the outcome can impact directly on their lives; they therefore have an incentive to become informed about the issues. And the information can be packaged for the electors in a simple and user-friendly fashion, including through the Internet.

overall assessment

How should we assess the legislative referendum and the constitutional initiative against the criteria we set for citizen participation in government? On the positive side are some very clear advantages. Citizens have real power to determine the course of legislation, and are more directly engaged in, and informed about, the policy process as a result. The relationship between voters and elected representatives is significantly altered, with representatives having to be more directly responsive to the anticipated reactions of their constituents. Everyone can in principle take part, not just a selected few, so that the benefits of a more informed citizen body are spread as widely as possible. There are also plentiful opportunities for a more active citizen engagement, in collecting petition signatures and campaigning in the referendum itself. The associational life of civil society does not bypass the electoral process, but works through it.

On the downside, the quality of serious deliberation is quite patchy, both as between citizens and between issues: the more serious or divisive the issue, the more incentive there is to become informed, and the more attentive people are likely to be to face-to-face debate, if only through the medium of television or radio phone-ins. And, as with all elections, mass referenda are dependent for their outcomes on the financial resources that can be mobilised in support, and especially on business sponsorship, which may have its own interests to pursue. So the principle of political equality is by no means fully preserved.

How far could the practices of Switzerland and the US states be generalised? In principle, there is no reason why they should not be applicable anywhere. Objections from elected politicians that referenda would undermine the integrity or coherence of the representative process are largely self-serving concerns about the inconvenience it might bring to their legislative programmes and to their monopoly of the legislative process. In a period when respect for parliamentary representation is at such a low level, the introduction of a right of citizen initiative could provide a much needed 'shot in the arm', as well as produce a much closer and more collaborative relationship between citizens and their representatives.

digital democracy

There is an important distinction to be made between the idea of digital democracy – also known as electronic democracy (e-democracy), virtual democracy, cyberdemocracy etc. – and the other modes of reviving democracy we have so far considered in this chapter. This is that its basis is a *technology* of communication, involving the Internet and other computer-based applications, which is market-driven, and not intentionally democratic. Some argue that the technology is entirely neutral, and could as readily be used by governments for increased surveillance and control as by citizens for their own communication. Yet a plausible case could be made for concluding that the technology has an inherent bias towards empowering the citizen, in the following ways:

- It enables information of all kinds about government to be directly accessible to citizens in their own homes.
- It radically increases the speed of communication, while cutting its cost to virtually nothing, so facilitating contact and organisation between citizens.
- It is an interactive medium, which facilitates new forms of discussion and debate that transcend all spatial limitations.
- It is beyond the control of governments, whether control of its use or its development, and it makes national borders and censorships largely irrelevant.

Now, of course, such advantages can benefit uncivil groups (criminal gangs, paedophiles, neo-Nazis etc.) as well as civil or democratic ones, but this is a small price to pay for the wider democratic potential of the technology. Much more serious from a democratic point of view is that all its advantages are dependent upon the ability to access it, and that this ability is very unequally distributed between citizens. The greater the empowering capacity of the technology, the greater the deprivation for those who cannot access or use it. This is a point I shall return to later.

Given the Internet's democratic potential, it has been seen as possibly inaugurating a new form of direct democracy in cyberspace, bypassing the terrestrial institutions of representative democracy altogether. This is a wildly exaggerated fantasy. Most of the democratic applications to date have taken the form of *reviving* or *enhancing* the established processes of representative democracy, rather than *transcending* them. In any case, as we have already seen, the sharp antithesis between direct and representative democracy is misconceived, since the direct involvement of citizens in the political process in different ways is necessary if representative institutions are to function in a democratic manner.

There is another antithesis relating to the new technology that is also often overstated: between e-government and e-democracy. The former, it is said, is top-down, the latter bottom-up. Certainly, some government uses of information technology may not be particularly democratic or democracy-enhancing. Yet most democratic governments have taken initiatives to put their documents on-line, to make information about public services and entitlements accessible electronically, and to solicit voters' opinions on a whole range of issues. Increased governmental accountability and responsiveness do not just depend on citizen activism; they require a certain reciprocity on the part of government itself. Moreover, only government is able to reduce the inequalities of resources and capacity in relation to the new technology which the market merely reproduces, if not actually intensifies.

These points can be best developed by looking briefly at the many different ways in which digital technology has been used to renew and strengthen the democratic character of representative institutions and processes.

dissemination of information

This is not just a matter of the ready availability of information that governments choose to disclose. It is also about the rapid dissemination of information which a government would much prefer not to have disclosed. Two examples from the Iraq war will suffice, one from the UK, and the other from the USA. When the independent Hutton enquiry into the death of weapons expert Dr David Kelly decided to post all its evidence and documentation on the Web, including e-mails between members of the government, the effect was enormous. It not only revealed the inner workings of government in quite a new way, but it enabled conclusions to be drawn about the 'dodgy dossiers' on Iraq's weapons of mass destruction which were diametrically opposed to those drawn by Lord Hutton himself. Even more dramatic than this was the unofficial circulation on the Internet of pictorial evidence of abuse committed by US forces in Abu Ghraib jail, which caused much greater shock even than the detailed verbal descriptions of the events.

Both examples serve to explode a common myth about the Internet: that as a direct form of communication it can come to replace the more traditional media. It was only when the Web material from Hutton and Abu Ghraib was reproduced in the newspapers and on television that it came to have a fully public impact; now it could simply not be ignored. The Internet communities are largely fragmented and specialised communities, and it requires the traditional media, for all their inadequacies, to give them wider public resonance. With regard to documentary material, in particular, journalists and other experts are needed to select and interpret the increasing volume of Web material; so these established intermediaries become more, not less, essential in the new information age.

ease of access to representatives

It is much easier to communicate with one's elected representative by e-mail than by any of the traditional means: surface mail, telephone or attending a constituency 'surgery'. In this regard, the technology enhances the connection between representatives and their voters. How far it makes them more *responsive*, however, is more doubtful, since replies tend to come in the form of stock answers developed for general circulation, which often do not address the precise questions asked. This is also the conclusion of studies of the most ambitious on-line system of voter communication to date, that of the Clinton White House. They show that e-mail provided a wholly new means of access for voters to the White House, but that, with messages forwarded to the relevant department for standard replies, little evidence of enhanced voter influence could be found as a result. This experience suggests that the technology itself cannot alter the basic pattern of relationship between voters and public officials, but merely reproduces it. In any case, voters can have little influence on their own, compared with an organised group, and it is more likely in its facilitation of group interaction that the Internet can make a difference.

enhanced voter discrimination

Most established communication with the voters by election candidates and parties takes the form of short TV sound bites and negative advertising. Websites allow candidates to provide much fuller information on their policy positions, and to respond directly to voters' enquiries about them. In the USA, a number of independent on-line sites have been developed, which promote debate and assessment of candidates in a more systematic way. Minnesota E-Democracy is an on-line forum which has pioneered discussions and debates with candidates since the 1994 election. In California, the Democracy Network (DNet) has developed a system for the online comparison of candidates' positions across a range of key issues, including lesser candidates who do not have websites of their own. Such initiatives contribute to a more informed electorate, by providing information which is necessarily more impartial than the candidates' own.

on-line citizens' forums

Arguably the most significant democratic potential of digital technology lies in lateral or horizontal communication between citizens, rather than vertical communication with government. This falls broadly into two categories: discussion and deliberation sites, and action sites, though naturally there is some overlap between the two. Discussion sites can relate to general democratic issues, such as Minnesota E-Democracy already mentioned, or Open Democracy based in the UK. Or they may be subject-specific, devoted to any of the multitude of issues which are matters of public policy or current concern. Studies of these sites indicate that relatively few of those who log onto these sites actually contribute to these discussions, so the level of active as opposed to passive participation may not be as great as the overall numbers suggest.

activist sites

One of the most distinctive features of the Internet is the capacity it affords to inform and mobilise large numbers of activists for campaigns, demonstrations and other events at short notice. Two very different examples will illustrate this. One is the massive global demonstrations against the Iraq war of 15 February 2003, which generated the numbers they did, especially of young people, largely through Internet communication. The other is the US presidential primary campaign of Howard Dean in 2003–4, which energised a whole new generation of activists again through a campaign website and informal e-mail communication between activists.

Although from one point of view both campaigns could be said to have 'failed', they both changed the face of politics. The Iraq demonstrations contributed to a global public opinion against the war, which denied it the legitimacy of UN endorsement. Howard Dean's campaign reinvigorated the grass roots of party politics, and demonstrated that there was a popular radical alternative to the official Democrat acquiescence in the Bush agenda. Both campaigns have also left ongoing e-networks of activists: in Britain for anti-racist and civil liberties campaigns; in the USA for progressive groups within the Democrat Party under a Democracy for America banner.

inequalities of access

Two broad conclusions can be drawn from the different democratic uses of the Internet reviewed above. The first is that the new technology enhances, but does not radically change, existing patterns of activity and relationship within representative politics. The second is that it does little to increase the direct influence of voters on their representatives. Where it has the greatest impact is in the ease of access to, and dissemination of, information, and in the lateral communication between citizens, both for deliberation and especially for political action.

From a democratic point of view, however, the most worrying aspect of the new technology is the sharp inequalities between those who have access to its facilities and those who are excluded. Exclusions can be of different kinds. People may be unable to afford a computer or service provider in the first place. They may be able to afford them, but be unable to use them. They may be able to use them, but not their full search facilities or interactive capabilities. Or they may be able to use these, but have no interest in doing so for any political purpose. These exclusions follow the pattern of existing non-participation in politics, being related to low income and educational attainment. The only point where they differ is that, where the elderly are much more likely to vote than the young, it is the latter who are much more likely to use digital technology than the former. Digital democracy, we might conclude, enfranchises the young.

overall assessment

How, then, does digital democracy perform against our criteria of participation? It is difficult to answer this question categorically, since so much depends upon the context. Here, I come back to our point of departure. The Internet is a technology of communication, not a mode of political activity or engagement in itself. It does not create new forms of direct democracy or of political action and influence where these do not already exist. But for those who can access the technology, what it does do is to significantly lower the cost threshold of participating, and in mobilising others to participate, whatever form this may take: accessing or disseminating information, contacting a representative or government official, deliberating with others, or taking part in a political campaign. And, of course, the technology removes the limitation of space, so that face-to-face communication can be replicated without leaving the comfort of one's home. So the technology certainly produces a widening of participation as a result. However, this is so only within the category of those who have access to it, which is limited even within the developed countries. And when one considers that less than five per cent of the population in most developing countries has access to the Internet, the full possibilities of digital democracy still lie very much in the future.

conclusion

The four modes of participation reviewed in this chapter illustrate different ways in which citizens can be involved directly in the work of government. They are not alternatives to the representative process; they are, rather, attempts to combat the perceived failures of representatives to engage with citizens or to address their needs. Nor do they replace more traditional ways in which citizens in a democracy have always sought to engage with governments: through interest and pressure groups; through single-issue campaigns; through mass demonstrations, and so on. What they demonstrate is the need for a continual renewal of democratic politics *from below*, if the representative process is not to fall prey to the oligarchic tendencies to which it is so often prone.

further reading

Barber, Benjamin. *Strong Democracy*. Berkeley and Los Angeles: University of California Press, 1984.

Budge, Ian. *The New Challenge of Direct Democracy*. Cambridge: Polity Press, 1996.

Butler, David and Austin Ranney. *Referendums around the World*. Basingstoke: Macmillan, 1994.

Fishkin, James. *Democracy and Deliberation*. New Haven and London: Yale University Press, 1991.

Fishkin, James. *The Voice of the People*. New Haven and London: Yale University Press, 1995.

Fung, Archon and Erik Olin Wright, eds. *Deepening Democracy*. London and New York: Verso, 2003.

Hacker, Kenneth and Jan van Dijk, eds. *Digital Democracy*. London and Thousand Oaks CA: Sage Publications, 2001.

Norris, Pippa. *Digital Divide: Civic Engagement, Information Poverty and the Internet Worldwide*. Cambridge: Cambridge University Press, 2001.

Stewart, John, Elizabeth Kendall and Anna Coote. *Citizens' Juries*. London: Institute for Public Policy Research, 1994.

Wainwright, Hilary. *Reclaim the State: Experiments in Popular Democracy*. London and New York: Verso, 2003.

conclusion: getting active

The previous chapter serves to reinforce two conclusions about democracy which have been present as themes throughout the book. First, democracy is a collective or social practice, involving discussion, argument and debate in the course of reaching an agreed decision and engaging in action with others. Although some features of democracy appear quite individualistic, such as the secret personal choice involved in voting, or the defence of an individual's rights by the courts, these turn out on closer inspection to be collective in nature. Voting is nothing if not a collective activity, carried out simultaneously with others to determine who will hold public office on our common behalf. And the individual rights which form the core of democracy are precisely those necessary for citizens to interact freely with others – the freedoms of expression, association, assembly, and so on. These are essentially collective rights, even though they have to be guaranteed to individuals if they are to be fully protected.

A second theme of the book is that the institutions of representative democracy become an empty shell without the constant activity and engagement of ordinary citizens between election time. Without this, politicians become even more detached in their separate world, and feel themselves beyond the reach of public accountability. This in turn reinforces a further cycle of apathy and alienation on the part of the public at large. Conscientious politicians may seek to break out of this cycle by experimenting with new ways of engaging with their public, but in the end democratic renewal only comes through popular mobilisation from below, just as it was only through struggle from below that our core democratic rights were won and made secure in the first place. So it is up to us.

Many political scientists operate with a highly economistic conception of human nature and dispositions: we are all self-interest maximisers or 'satisficers', always ready to calculate what course of action will be most beneficial to us. On this basis, it becomes hard to explain how any public action for a common purpose ever takes place at all. Even if an outcome will be beneficial to us (e.g. campaigning for cleaner streets), the 'rational' individual will calculate that the individual benefit will never be sufficient to compensate him or her for the time and effort expended. Much better to leave it to others, and enjoy the benefits anyway. Unfortunately, if such a calculation is generalised, absolutely nothing will get done and no benefits will ever materialise.

To be sure, we do not live in a highly public-oriented culture, such as was celebrated by Pericles in Athens of the fifth century BCE, or by Tocqueville in nineteenth-century America. This is how Pericles described his contemporary Athens: 'Here each individual is interested not only in his own affairs, but in the affairs of state as well … we do not say that a man who takes no interest in politics is a man who minds his own business; we say that he has no business here at all.' Or this from Tocqueville: 'It is hard to explain the place filled by political concerns in the life of an American. To take a hand in the government of society and to talk about it is his most important business . . If an American should be reduced to occupying himself with his own affairs, at that moment half his existence would be snatched from him.'

Our contemporary culture is not like that. It is much more individualistic and privatised, and Mrs Thatcher and President Reagan did their best to turn us all into the very model of interest-maximising economizers, each in our own private realm. Yet their own activity as politicians at least questioned the universal validity of their assumptions. The same is true of the political thinker in the eighteenth to nineteenth centuries who was most strenuous in asserting narrow self-interest as the universal driver of human action, Jeremy Bentham. How, then, could he explain his own life so completely dedicated to public improvement?

The fact is that strong elements of a public-oriented culture still coexist with the more individualist and privatised ones. After all, we are social animals, and much satisfaction as well as benefit can come from helping to realise some collective purpose with others. Naturally, such a public disposition is much stronger in some people than others, and their contribution is crucial to keep the democratic processes described in this book going. If you have reached this far in the book, you are probably one of these. Well, you don't have to content yourself with just reading about democracy; you can also practise it, if you don't already. Here are some suggestions: @ to PB list

- Start local. What upsets or annoys you about your immediate environment? Contact your local council or elected representative. Better still, find out if there is a local group which specialises in the issue – a civic society, amenity group, a police-liaison network, or whatever. Use Yellow Pages, Internet search, a council enquiries or complaints line.
- Join an on-line forum or discussion group, either on a specific subject that concerns you, or a general democracy site. Try the Open Democracy forum (www.opendemocracy.net) or search for a site through the Democracies Online Newsletter (www.e-democracy.org/do/).
- Join a national democracy or human rights organisation, and see if it has a branch in your town or city. Amnesty International, national civil liberties organisations, solidarity campaigns with oppressed peoples in different parts of the world – many of these have local branches where you can become more actively involved.
- Join a union at your place of work. If there isn't one, find out who else thinks there should be. There's safety in numbers. If you are a shareholder, make sure you know what the company policy is on key issues, and if possible attend the annual shareholders' meeting.
- If you are a student, join your year or school council, or college union, or whatever opportunities for direct and representative democracy are on offer. Learn how to handle debate and disagreement, and how to thrash out practical proposals for the general benefit. Start young and you won't regret it.
- Go on a demonstration. There's nothing like it for shaking out the cobwebs, and expressing some of that anger. If it is a regional or national demo, find out local transport arrangements so that you can travel with others, and have a singsong on the way back.
- Volunteer for some activity that is necessary to keep the social wheels turning – a parent–teachers' association, school gov.

governors, voluntary welfare agency, or whatever. You may have skills that could be put to good use.

- Join a political party. Yes, even that! Only don't allow yourself to become merely election fodder, or preoccupied with passing end-less resolutions to be sent up the line, where they only get shunted into a siding. Keep your elected representatives under pressure.
- Maybe you are time poor and money rich. In that case, subscribe to as many campaigns and organisations you sympathise with as you can. Much scorn is levelled at 'cheque-book participation', but it's important to support others to act on your behalf if you haven't the time to act yourself. Then you can always raise a cheer from your armchair, when you discover from a news bulletin that an organisation you support has been in the thick of the action.
- Never pass up an opportunity to vote, whatever sort of election, in whatever context. Remember the old adage: 'It is necessary only for the good to do nothing for evil to triumph.'

You've probably guessed it by now. I'm a committed activist myself! I'm just like one of the Americans Tocqueville describes, who would feel deprived of half of his existence if he were confined to purely pri-vate affairs. So let me finish by telling you about two of the things I am currently active in.

I am a fair-weather cyclist. Near where I live in Manchester there is what is claimed to be the longest urban cycleway in Britain, recently constructed by a national cycling organisation along the course of an old railway. I am a member of the cycleway support group, founded to encourage the use of the cycleway, to help main-tain it, and to press for improvements both to the track and to cycling facilities more generally in the city. We started with quite a narrow agenda, but soon found that we were liaising with various amenity groups along the route of the track, with environmentalists to develop a wildlife corridor, with schools along the route to encourage its use by students, and so on. My own contribution is modest and not very time-consuming: attending bi-monthly meet-ings, taking part in organised cycle rides, and acting as warden for a small stretch of the route to keep it free of glass and other debris. This may seem like very small beer. Yet it taps into much larger issues – the environment, health, urban mobility, recreation – and we have the satisfaction of seeing tangible results for our efforts.

A second activity is at the national level. I belong to an organis-ation or network called Democratic Audit, based at the University of

Essex, which conducts regular audits of the state of democracy in the UK. Our latest audit, entitled *Democracy under Blair*, is itemised in the further reading for chapter two. We have also been involved with an international organisation in Stockholm, the International Institute for Democracy and Electoral Assistance (IDEA), in developing a method and framework which can be used by citizens of any country to audit their own democracy. The point of such an audit is to identify the most significant strengths and weaknesses, as a contribution to reforming and strengthening the democratic process. We have published a step-by-step guide to auditing democracy in the form of a handbook, so that it can be used by citizen groups anywhere (*The International IDEA Handbook on Democracy Assessment*, Kluwer Law International, 2002; it is also available on the Democratic Audit and International IDEA websites – www.democraticaudit.com, www.idea.int). You might like to try out the questionnaire version of the framework, to see how much you know about your own country's democracy! It is organised very much according to the structure I have used in chapter 2.

The future of democracy, in conclusion, depends on ourselves. Democratic arrangements in practice, as I have already argued, involve a compromise between popular forces and powerful interests in economy, society and state. This compromise is rarely a stable one; the gravitational pull is always towards the interests of the powerful, unless there is a strong countervailing force on the other side. That countervailing force is an informed and alert citizen body, active at all levels of public life.

glossary of key terms

accountability This is a condition whereby those who hold an office or position of authority of any kind are required to give a regular account of their performance to an appropriate body, and are subject to a sanction if they have breached the terms of their position or have failed in some clearly defined way. A democratically elected government is accountable to a number of different bodies: to a parliament or legislature for its financial and political conduct; to the courts for the legality of its actions, and to public opinion for any aspect of its performance. Underpinning all these is its accountability to the electorate, which can exercise the ultimate sanction of dismissal from office. While a government's accountability to parliament and the courts are examples of what is called *lateral* accountability, its reckoning at the hands of the electorate from below is called *vertical* accountability.

bill of rights This is a written list of basic democratic rights which are legally guaranteed to all citizens. Besides the freedoms of expression, association and assembly, and the right to vote, which are necessary to democratic participation, a bill of rights will also typically safeguard the life and liberty of the citizen against arbitrary executive action or interference. If these rights are infringed, citizens can appeal to the courts for restitution or redress, even where a government may have been acting with majority support. In this way, a bill of rights serves to protect unpopular minorities or points of view in the face of majority disapproval. The objection that unelected judges are behaving undemocratically if they oppose the actions of a popularly elected government is not persuasive if what they are upholding are the fundamental rights and freedoms of every citizen as an equal member of a democratic society.

citizens' initiative A constitutional device whereby citizens can propose new laws themselves if they can secure a sufficient proportion of the electorate to sign a petition in favour. The proposal is then put to a vote or referendum of all citizens, and, if passed, becomes law. Constitutional provision for this device currently exists only in Italy, Switzerland and about half the states of the USA. In Switzerland, initiatives have to take the form of a constitutional amendment, and can be voted on at any time; in the USA, initiatives are voted on at the same time as the regular elections to public office. The citizens' initiative has been advocated more widely as a means to address the current malaise of representative democracy by reducing the gap between representatives and their electorate.

citizens' jury An arrangement for consulting citizens on policy, whereby a small socially representative group is selected to undertake an intensive examination and discussion of a policy issue over several days. The 'jury' will question expert witnesses, debate alternative proposals and arrive at a recommendation by consensus or majority vote. The recommendation is not binding on the sponsoring body, which may be government itself at national or local level. However, the arrangement comes close to an ideal form of deliberative democracy, in which participants' initial opinions come to be modified by informed debate, but without the distorting influence of party or special interests typical in a representative assembly. Their recommendations thus have considerable legitimacy, and can be useful to government when faced by a particularly difficult or controversial policy decision. Citizens' juries are similar to deliberative opinion polls, though these latter tend to have much larger numbers, and include consideration of candidates for public office as well as policy questions.

civil society This is the term given to the sphere of social interaction, separate from both state and economy, within which citizens communicate with one another directly and via different media, and organise collectively to meet a variety of purposes. A vigorous associational life in civil society is seen as a keystone of democracy, because it enables citizens to develop and articulate opinions independently of government, to work collectively to solve their own problems, and to bring pressure to bear on government across the whole range of policy. The concept of civil society was given renewed currency in the twentieth century as a contrast to the totalitarian regimes of fascism and communism, which sought to incorporate and supervise all associational life under the aegis of the state. The term 'civil' conveys the idea not only of a public sphere independent of the state, but also of one conforming to the norms of 'civility', i.e. respecting the rights of others and acting within the law.

consociational democracy Sometimes also known as 'consensus' democracy, this describes a type of political arrangement that developed in some European countries as a means of resolving deep social cleavages, where a pure majoritarian system would give permanent power to one social group over another. Its typical features comprise: a grand coalition or power-sharing executive; a mutual veto over key issues; a proportional electoral system, and a high level of autonomy for the different social segments. Examples have been Belgium, the Netherlands and Switzerland, and more recently the Belfast Agreement in Northern Ireland. Consociational arrangements are often prescribed as a model for deeply divided societies because they foster reconciliation and give all major groups a stake in the polity. Their disadvantage, however, is that they tend to rigidify social cleavages, and make it difficult for the electorate to 'turn the rascals out' of office.

corruption This is the practice of public office-holders abusing their position for private gain. It can take many forms, from the petty corruption of public service providers demanding an unauthorised payment at the point of service, to the huge backhanders demanded by those who control the award of public licences and contracts. Corruption undermines democracy in a number of ways. It distorts public priorities, by channelling investment into projects where the rewards of corruption are largest and easiest to conceal. It breaches the trust between the people and their elected politicians. And it undermines confidence that the electoral process can be used to change people's lives for the better, rather than feather the nests of those elected. Corruption is much more prevalent in developing than developed countries, partly because of limited economic opportunities outside the public sphere and inadequate salaries within it, and partly because of the absence of a strong culture of public service and public interest. However, it is also colluded in by businesses in the developed world, in their eagerness to secure lucrative contracts abroad.

cosmopolitan democracy This term refers to a body of thought which holds that, since many of the forces that shape people's conditions of life have moved beyond national borders, so democratic arrangements to control them can no longer be confined to the nation state, but must become supranational. The cosmopolitan ideal embodies a number of components: democratising existing international institutions to make them more representative and accountable; developing new mechanisms for the participation and representation of peoples, and not just states, at the supranational level; acknowledging different levels of overlapping citizenship at local, national, regional and global levels; extending the reach and legal enforceability of human rights regimes, and so on. Without extending democracy in this way, it is argued, it will become increasingly irrelevant, as purely national decision making becomes superseded by the global reach of economic, environmental, health and public security problems.

democracy A way of arranging decision making for a group or collectivity, involving open deliberation in which all members have an equal right to a voice and a vote. Where, for reasons of time and space, members agree that it is impractical for them to take decisions themselves, democracy may be realised through the election of representatives to take decisions on their behalf. For such an arrangement not to degenerate into oligarchy, however, a number of conditions have to be met. Members must be guaranteed an equal right to vote, to stand for elective office, to engage freely in political or campaigning activity, and to hold their representatives continuously to account. They should have full and accurate information about the reasons for decisions taken on their behalf. And they should have the right to change the terms of the relationship between themselves and their representatives. These conditions provide the rationale for the typical institutions of a modern representative democracy. They also provide the standard against which the democratic character of these institutions should be judged.

democratic consolidation This is a process whereby a democratic system of government becomes irreversible because its different institutional components have become firmly embedded and publicly valued. It follows an initial process of democratic transition, which consists in the replacement of a non-democratic regime with one based on electoral choice under conditions of free and fair competition. Consolidation is necessarily a more long-drawn-out process than that of transition, and there are no agreed tests to determine when it has been accomplished. The first replacement of a ruling party after the founding elections is neither a necessary nor a sufficient condition, though the recognition by political élites that elections constitute 'the only game in town' is an important element. Yet subsequent elections may not be genuinely free and fair, and other key democratic features are necessary to make them so: the transparency and accountability of government between elections; the guarantee of the rule of law and basic freedoms; the independence of the courts from the executive, and so on. Ultimately, democratic consolidation depends on a settled conviction among the electorate that having a choice of government makes a tangible difference to their daily lives.

democratic deficit The term describes a condition in which political arrangements are so lacking in one or other feature of democracy that it has become a matter of widespread public acknowledgement and concern. This may be because of a marked lack of transparency or accountability on the part of decision makers, or some chronic distortion of representation, or the virtual disengagement of the electorate or large sections of it from the political process. The idea of democratic deficit first became current in relation to the European Union, which was perceived to be deficient in all these respects. It has subsequently been used in relation to international organisations, and then to various features of individual states. Although it is possible to make a systematic assessment of any regime's democratic performance against international standards of best practice, e.g. through a democratic audit, the basis of such assessments will always be controversial. What is needed for some deficiency to become characterised as a 'democratic deficit' is the additional element of widespread public acknowledgement and concern.

devolution This is a process whereby functions of government are transferred downwards from the national centre to regional and local levels. Devolved government is held to be more democratic because it is closer to the people and more responsive to their needs. In federal systems, such as the USA, Australia, Brazil or India, individual states of the federation already enjoy considerable autonomy. In unitary states, however, processes of increasing centralisation have been difficult to resist, partly in the name of equality of citizen rights and service provision throughout the country, and partly to secure central economic and fiscal management. Yet the alternative principle of subsidiarity – that public services should be devolved to the level at which they can be most responsively and effectively delivered – is currently gaining ground. From a democratic point of view, much depends on the extent to which local units of government and service provision are themselves democratically representative, responsive and accountable.

digital democracy This term denotes the use of electronic information and communication media to enhance the political knowledge and participation of citizens, and to enrich the democratic process more generally. Recent advances in communication technology have been hailed as empowering citizens in relation to both their elected representatives and the traditional media, by enabling them to communicate directly and cheaply with one another without spatial limits, thus creating a 'virtual democracy' of quite a new kind. Such claims may be exaggerated. Electronic means of communication are best seen as complementing rather than replacing existing political and media channels. While in this respect they clearly enhance democratic opportunities, they cannot do so for social groups which tend to be excluded from the electronic conversation – the poor and elderly in developed countries, and the ninety-five per cent of the population in most developing countries who have no access to the Internet.

direct democracy This exists wherever members of an association are able to decide on public issues themselves, rather than by electing representatives to decide on their behalf ('representative democracy'). It was the form of democracy used in the ancient Greek world, in Swiss cantons and in New England town meetings, and it was held to be the only form of democracy until systems of representative government came to be developed in the eighteenth century and the franchise extended in the nineteenth and twentieth centuries. Nowadays, it is assumed that direct democracy can only be practised in the small associations of civil society, rather than at the level of government. Yet the existence of referenda and citizens' initiatives, as well as the revival of citizen assemblies at local level, shows that it is perfectly possible for ordinary citizens to take considered decisions themselves on important policy issues. And we should not forget a classic example of direct democracy in the jury system, where twelve men and women have the power to decide the fate of their fellow citizens – a task that everyone is likely to have to perform at some point in their lives.

due process This refers to the legal safeguards designed to protect potential criminal suspects from arbitrary or oppressive detention and, when charged with an offence, to ensure them a fair trial. Such safeguards include the right not to be held beyond a specified time without charge, the right of confidential access to a lawyer of one's own choosing, the right to be treated as innocent until proved guilty in a properly constituted court, and so on. The importance of legal due process to democracy lies especially in the protection it affords to political opponents of a government from arbitrary or oppressive detention, or extra-legal harassment of all kinds.

engendering democracy This is the term given to strategies for improving the low participation rates of women in political office and public life more generally, and in making conditions of work more amenable to them. These strategies include: affirmative action policies in public recruitment and promotion agencies, and in candidate selection by political parties; providing adequate childcare facilities and making hours of work more family-friendly, and in changing embedded institutional cultures. From a democratic point of view, it matters if any section of society is markedly privileged or disprivileged in access to public office, whether elected or non-elected. There is also good reason to suppose that issues affecting women are not taken so seriously by men, or given sufficient priority in the competition for public funding. In any case, society as a whole is poorer if the distinctive attributes and qualities developed by women are not given due scope in public life.

executive The executive, sometimes known simply as 'the government', comprises all government ministers and public officials, including the police and law enforcement officers. In a parliamentary system, government ministers are drawn from parliament, whereas in a pure presidential system such as the USA, they are appointed from outside the legislature. In a mixed system, as in France, they are mainly appointed from the national assembly, although the president, as head of the executive, is elected separately. All democracies follow the principle of the separation of powers, whereby the three branches of state – executive, legislature and judiciary – have separate functions: the executive, to decide and execute policy and implement the law; the legislature, to approve legislation and hold the executive to account; the judiciary, to adjudicate and enforce the law in the courts. In a parliamentary system, the separation of powers is more blurred than in a presidential one, since the initiative for legislation lies almost wholly with the elected government ministers, and parliament has less independence in holding the executive to account.

free and fair elections The principle that elections in a democracy should be 'free and fair' is now well established, as are also the international standards governing what this means in practice. These standards cover everything from the registration of parties, candidates and voters, through the conduct of the election itself, to the counting of ballots and the procedure for disputes and appeals. 'Freedom' requires that candidates and parties remain unimpeded in organising and communicating with the electors; 'fairness' requires a level playing-field in access to state facilities and public service media, and the oversight of the electoral process by an impartial electoral commission. However, a truly level field can never be realised in practice because of the operation of informal factors, such as an inequality of resources, or the initiative that lies with governing parties in the period before an election. Moreover, the electoral system itself may disadvantage some parties disproportionately.

freedom of information This is the principle that citizens, journalists and other interested parties should have the right of access to government documents, and governments have the duty to disclose them, and the legislation giving effect to this principle. Most FOI legislation in practice makes exceptions for sensitive personal information, for commercial secrets, for issues of national security, and for advice given to ministers in confidence. Any further exceptions than these make the legislation unduly restrictive, as in the current UK legislation, which contains no fewer than thirty-five separate categories of exception. Even where exceptions are limited, the freedom may be restricted in practice by the excessive cost of access, or by denying applicants the right of appeal to the courts in the event of non-disclosure.

globalisation In its original meaning, globalisation denotes a process whereby economic activities, trade and finance have increasingly expanded across national borders and become global. With the lowering of transport costs and the speed of modern communication, companies can locate themselves wherever conditions are most profitable, and financiers can transfer huge capital sums across borders in a moment. Although globalisation is partly a product of technical changes, it was given a huge impetus by political decisions taken in Washington and London during the 1980s to press for the international deregulation of economic and financial activities. At a more general level, globalisation indicates an increasingly inter-dependent world, in which activities in one country have significant effects in another, whether in terms of the environment, migration, criminality or the spread of disease. One important consequence is that national governments are less able to control the conditions that matter for the welfare of their citizens, and can only do so through international co-operation and global institutions. Democracy has itself to go global as a result.

interest groups This term refers to any group sharing similar ideas or interests which is organised in the public arena to promote its ends, whether through pressure on government or through influencing public opinion. Traditional democratic theorists saw such groups as sectional and divisive, and some sought to ban them altogether, but they have proved to be an essential component of democratic politics. Citizens can only exercise any political influence by joining with like-minded others, and the plurality of interest groups simply reflects the complex diversity of contemporary societies. Commentators frequently make a distinction between 'private interest' groups, such as trade union or business organisations, which exist to protect and promote the interests of their members, and 'public interest' groups, which promote causes in the wider public interest, such as civil liberties or environmental concerns. While interest groups are a natural product of the democratic freedoms of association and expression, they are more problematic from the standpoint of political equality, since marked differences in financial resources and access to government give some groups an influence out of all proportion to their membership numbers.

legislature The legislature, or parliament as it is called in a parliamentary system, or national assembly in the French tradition, is the key institution of representative democracy. It is where elected representatives, standing in for the people as a whole, meet to debate issues of national importance, to prepare and approve legislation, to agree on taxation and public expenditure, and to scrutinise the actions and policies of the executive. In a parliamentary system, the assembly also serves as a training and recruiting ground for future government ministers. Most democracies have a second or upper chamber of the legislature, whether elected or appointed, or a combination of the two, whose task is to act as a filter for legislation from the main or lower chamber, and, in a federal system, to represent the interests of the constituent states. Most of the work of a contemporary legislature is carried out in specialist committees, reflecting the often complex and technical nature of modern government. Some commentators believe that legislatures are increasingly losing importance as executives bypass them to engage directly with the media and special interests. Yet they remain the essential locus of popular legitimacy in the political process.

majoritarianism Counting heads to find where majority support lies is a basic feature of democratic decision making. It reflects the principle of political equality: everyone should count for one, and none for more than one. Deciding by majority vote is clearly much more democratic than allowing minorities to decide. However, it can leave minorities feeling impotent and alienated from the decisional process. There are two situations in particular where the majority procedure can become undemocratic. One is where it is used to infringe a minority's basic democratic rights and freedoms; the other is where the configuration of elections and parties gives permanent power to a majority social group, and a minority is excluded from any share or turn in government. Both situations infringe the principle of political equality on which the majority procedure is itself based. The solution is to institute more consensual forms of government and decision making. In any case, the search for consensus should be the first step in any democratic decisional procedure, using devices such as amendment and compromise; voting by the majority should come as a last, rather than first, resort, when agreement has proved impossible.

market democracy It is taken for granted today that democracy and a free-market economy belong together, and that they are mutually reinforcing. This is only partly true. Certainly, among basic freedoms is the right to exchange and trade freely with others. And a market economy sets limits to the power of the state by decentralising economic decisions, and by dispersing opportunities, information and resources within civil society. Yet the very domination of the market today has a number of negative consequences for democracy. It makes a country vulnerable to fluctuations in international finance and trade that deprive it of self-determination in economic policy. It intensifies economic inequalities in a way that can undermine the democratic principle of political equality. And, in privileging the consumer over the citizen, it elevates the private over the public interest, and the pursuit of individual choice above deliberation about collective goods. Historically, democratic government has been seen as the means for regulating, supplementing and redistributing market outcomes, rather than subordinating itself to them.

parliamentary and presidential systems In a parliamentary system, the head of government or prime minister is usually the leader of the largest party or coalition able to secure a majority in parliament, from whose members government ministers are also chosen. The head of state is a largely ceremonial office, and may be directly elected, indirectly elected by parliament, or appointed on a hereditary basis, as in a constitutional monarchy. In a presidential system, the president is both chief executive and head of state, and is elected independently of the legislature, appointing ministers from outside its ranks. Both systems can be equally democratic, though there are advantages and disadvantages to each. Because of the much clearer separation of powers in a presidential system, the legislature can act as a more effective check on the executive than in a parliamentary system. Yet this can lead to policy 'gridlock', in which a president cannot effect his or her electoral mandate. And in insecure democracies, presidents may resort to bypassing the legislature, curtailing its powers, or even dismissing it altogether in a constitutional *coup d'état*. Such a conflict is unlikely in a parliamentary system, where premiers owe their position to parliament, and have to work with it rather than against it. By the same token, parliament has much weaker checking powers, since the interest of a majority of its members lies in supporting the government rather than causing it embarrassment, and so giving comfort to the opposition.

political party In contrast to an interest group, a party is a membership organisation devoted to winning and holding public office. In a democracy, parties compete for electoral support by offering the voters a choice of leaders and programmes. Although they are often criticised for their tight internal discipline, there is an advantage to voters in knowing that the elected members of the party they have voted for are all committed to supporting a publicly declared policy agenda. Two other features are more significant in the current malaise of party politics. One is the rapidly diminishing difference between party programmes, as parties of the Left adjust to operating within the constraints of global capitalism. Offering more efficient political management is a poor substitute for a bold or distinctive policy platform, and reduces the incentive to the electorate to turn out to vote. A second and related feature is the decline in the internal democracy of parties, such that political activists find more scope for achievement in single-issue organisations and movements, which seek to influence policy rather than hold governmental office. It is too soon to sound the death-knell of parties, however. If they disappeared we should have to reinvent them, since it is only possible for the like-minded to have any political influence by combining together, whether in parliament or outside.

political representation This has two basic meanings. The first is an *agency* concept, whereby an elected representative is seen as authorised by, standing for, acting on behalf of, and accountable to, his or her constituents. This concept reflects the democratic principle that all political authority stems from the people, and is exercised on their sufferance. While electors cannot bind their representatives, the fact that they possess the regular sanction of dismissal sets limits to the representative's individual freedom of decision. The second concept of political representation is a *microcosmic* one, whereby the legislative assembly as a whole can be said to be representative to the extent that it reflects or mirrors the diverse character of the electorate in some relevant respect: its social composition; its geographical distribution, or the distribution of its political opinions. How far an assembly reflects the first of these (the social composition) depends on the priorities that political parties adopt in candidate selection. How far it reflects the other two depends on the nature of the electoral system. This microcosmic conception embodies the democratic principle of political equality, whether between voters, or in their access to public office.

proportional representation This is a principle for electoral systems which requires the distribution of the popular vote between the different parties, whether locally, regionally or nationally, to be reflected in the number of seats won. Its rationale is that a representative assembly should mirror as closely as possible the balance of political opinion in the country, as measured by the degree of support for the different parties. This purpose can be achieved in a number of ways. Under a *list* system, parties present a list of candidates in multi-member constituencies, and seats are distributed according to the number of votes cast for each party. Under a *mixed member* or *additional member* system, electors have two votes, one for a candidate in a single-member constituency and one for a party list. Once all constituency candidates have been elected, the remaining seats are distributed between the parties in such a way as to ensure that their overall tally of seats conforms as closely as possible to their share of the popular vote. Under the *single transferable vote*, again in multi-member constituencies, electors choose their candidates in order of preference, and the outcome will again be broadly proportionate to the degree of a party's popular support. In contrast to all these voting systems, the plurality system in single-member constituencies ('first past the post') can produce an assembly which is highly unrepresentative of the distribution of political opinion in the country. It also discriminates against smaller parties gaining any political representation at all.

public opinion Since voters have the ultimate power to dismiss a government through the electoral process, what they think of its performance and its policies between elections is of considerable significance. This is what constitutes public opinion. It can be most conveniently assessed through the sampling techniques of opinion polls, though these tend to tap into spontaneous reactions rather than considered judgements. Public opinion is formed in a number of different ways: through informal discussion; through the influence of the mass media; through the activity of interest and advocacy groups; through the contributions of independent experts, and of course through the government's own information efforts. Of these, the mass media are arguably the most important, though their claims to represent and not merely influence public opinion are often exaggerated.

referendum In contrast to elections, which determine the voters' choice of candidates for public office, a referendum gives voters the opportunity to decide directly on a legislative or constitutional issue. A government may be constitutionally required to hold a referendum whenever a change in the country's constitution is proposed. Or it may choose to call one as a way of settling a controversial issue on which it is itself divided. Or a referendum may be prompted by electors themselves, where the facility of a 'citizens' initiative' exists. Although in some countries the outcome of a referendum is not constitutionally binding on government, the fact that the people constitute the ultimate court of appeal in a democracy makes its verdict impossible to ignore. Some would argue that the people are not well enough informed to take decisions directly, and that referenda undermine the integrity of the representative process. However, the responsibility of deciding an important public issue gives people the incentive to become informed. And where the constitutional opportunity exists for the people either to veto legislation or to propose changes of their own, it prevents legislators from getting far out of touch with the views of the electorate.

rule of law The idea of the rule of law predates democracy, but is an essential component of it, since without it the laws passed by a popularly elected assembly will not be effectively implemented, or the persons and property of citizens be protected from arbitrary executive interference. The rule of law embodies a number of requirements. All law should be certain, and its provisions and penalties be known in advance. No one should be above the law, whatever their position or social standing, and all should be equal before it. In particular, all public officials should be subject to the law, and act within the terms of legally prescribed duties and procedures, including the constitutionally protected rights of citizens. For these requirements to be enforceable, the judiciary has to be institutionally independent of both executive and legislature, and personally incorruptible, so that it can interpret and enforce the law without fear or favour. There also has to be extensive public provision of legal aid, if citizens are not to be denied access to the law or legal representation because of poverty.

selection by lot In classical Athenian democracy, the lot, or random selection, was regarded as a more democratic selection device than election for public bodies smaller than the whole citizen assembly. This is because the lot embodies the principle of political equality in its purest form: each citizen has an equal chance of being selected, and is regarded as equally competent as any other for the duties required. The Athenians used it for selection for jury service and for the rotating membership of the administrative Council. Today, its use is largely confined to jury service. For selection by lot to meet another requirement – that the body selected should form a cross-section of the citizen body as a whole – quite large numbers are needed. For this purpose, random selection can be combined with selection by representative sample, as in contemporary citizens' juries or deliberative opinion polls. This method has been suggested as an element in the reform of the UK's second chamber of parliament.

social democracy This was the self-description used by many parties of the Left in twentieth-century Europe, to characterise their political programmes of using power, democratically won, to modify market capitalism through a welfare state and social ownership of public utilities. In the contemporary world, social democracy can be seen as a necessary complement to political democracy, and refers to the guarantee of basic economic and social rights, without which democratic citizenship cannot be fully realised. Without health, education, housing, a guaranteed income, and so on, citizens will not be in a position to exercise their civil and political rights as equals. From this perspective, the provision of economic and social rights can be seen as a *condition* for political democracy, rather than just one possible *outcome* of it.

spin This recently coined term describes the practices of aggressive news management currently adopted by many elected governments. Governments have always sought to put the most favourable gloss on their activities as part of their task of public persuasion. What is new is the huge escalation in the numbers of government information officers, their degree of political co-ordination and the way in which no tactic is considered too low in the fight to secure a favourable headline or to hide information which might discredit the government. The apotheosis of 'spin' was represented by an e-mail circular within the UK transport ministry on 11 September 2001, to the effect that this was a 'good day to bury bad news'. Governments blame the hostility of the media for their difficulties in getting their message across. Yet their own connivance in the devious arts of spinning reinforces public distrust, and makes it difficult for them to have an adult conversation with their electorates, especially about the limits of their power. Concentrating on the message seems to serve as a compensation for an actual decline in government capacity.

transparency This is a quasi-technical term, equivalent to the older idea of open government. It is a condition of effective accountability of officials that those to whom they are accountable should have full and accurate information about what they are doing. In respect of government, this can best be secured by an effective freedom of information regime, and strong powers for legislators to require the disclosure of government documents.

universal suffrage That all adult citizens should have the right to an equal vote is a basic condition of representative democracy, and one that has only been achieved by persistent struggles on the part of those excluded to remove the legal and other obstacles to their electoral participation. Debates still take place over whether convicted criminals should be allowed to vote, and at what age young people are sufficiently mature to be admitted to full citizenship. Most of the significant exclusions that remain concern the difficulties that people experience in getting enrolled on the electoral register, and these figures rarely appear in the electoral statistics.

democracy and human rights organisations and websites

african centre for democracy and human rights studies

http://www1.umn.edu/humanrts/africa/ACOHRS.htm
The African Centre for Democracy and Human Rights Studies
(ACDHRS) is a regional Non-Governmental Organisation that promotes the observance of human and peoples' rights and democratic
principles throughout Africa. The ACDHRS facilitates dialogue
between African NGOs and their counterparts elsewhere, and runs
research, education and training programmes.

american civil liberties union

http://www.aclu.org
The American Civil Liberties Union (ACLU) campaigns for the
protection of civil liberties in the USA, supporting complainants/
defendants in courts and lobbying legislatures. The ACLU also
works to improve the rights of excluded groups, such as Native
Americans, ethnic minorities, the gay community, mental-health
patients, prisoners, people with disabilities and the poor.

amnesty international

http://www.amnesty.org

Amnesty International is a worldwide membership organisation with supporters and members in more than 150 countries. Amnesty works to promote all human rights, with a particular focus on undertaking research and action focused on civil and political rights – preventing and ending grave abuses of the rights to physical and mental integrity, freedom of conscience and expression, and freedom from discrimination. Its annual reports cover developments in most countries around the world.

article 19

http://www.article19.org

Article 19 takes its name from Article 19 of the Universal Declaration of Human Rights, which establishes the right to freedom of opinion and expression. Article 19 focuses its research and campaign work specifically on combating censorship by promoting freedom of expression, access to official information, and institutional and informal censorship. Article 19 has members in thirty countries worldwide.

carter centre

http://www.cartercenter.org

The Carter Centre funds and undertakes activities to support democracy and transition to democracy around the world. It engages in conflict prevention and mediation, education and training, electoral monitoring, disease prevention, socio-economic development, and works with refugees, among many other activities.

democratic audit

http://www.democraticaudit.com

Democratic Audit is a research and advocacy organisation that promotes understanding and discussion of democracy and democratic processes in Britain and internationally. Democratic Audit has published three major 'audits' of democracy in the UK, which evaluate how the practice of democracy in Britain compares with ideal or best practice elsewhere. The concept of democratic audit is also used by similar, independent organisations in Sweden, Australia and the United States.

freedom house

http://www.freedomhouse.org
Freedom House advocates for and supports the development of democracy abroad through lobbying and campaign work, and by running international democratisation training programmes. Freedom House publishes an annual report ranking the level of freedom enjoyed in most countries around the world.

human rights watch

http://www.hrw.org
Human Rights Watch campaigns for better protection for human rights around the world. Its professional staff conduct fact-finding missions to better understand the scale and nature of human rights abuse in particular trouble spots around the world. HRW actively follows developments in more than seventy countries and produces authoritative and detailed reports on human rights abuse in the United States and Europe, as well as in developing countries.

initiative and referendum institute europe

http://www.iri-europe.org
The premier research and educational institute on public initiatives and referendums in Europe.

initiative and referendum institute, university of southern california

http://www.iandrinstitute.org
The premier research and educational institute on public initiatives and referendums in the USA.

institute for democracy in south africa

http://www.idasa.org.za
The Institute for Democracy in South Africa (Idasa) works to build capacity for democracy in civil society and government in South

Africa. Its main areas of activity are: improving understanding of electoral representation and community and public participation; highlighting the importance of public services and of appropriately articulated demands from citizens, and promoting understanding of the role of the law.

international centre for trade union rights

http://www.ictur.org
Organising and campaigning for the improvement and defence of trade union rights around the world, the International Centre for Trade Union Rights provides a focal point for trade unionists, labour lawyers and academics worldwide.

international foundation for election systems

http://www.ifes.org
The International Foundation for Election Systems is a non-governmental organisation that provides support for election administration and management. In addition to training, advice and election monitoring, the IFES also develops programmes to strengthen the rule of law, encourage good governance and promote participation by civil society.

international idea

http://www.idea.int
International IDEA (The International Institute for Democracy and Electoral Assistance) is an agency supported by twenty-one member governments with a commitment to promoting democracy and democratic practices. IDEA's interests lie in strengthening electoral processes, encouraging the development of political parties, and promoting political equality and participation.

international press institute

http://www.freemedia.at
International Press Institute is dedicated to the promotion and protection of press freedom and the improvement of the practices of journalism. It has an extensive network of members in over one hundred countries, who provide support to journalists threatened by governments or individuals for their reporting.

inter-parliamentary union

http://www.ipu.org
The Inter-Parliamentary Union (IPU) is the focal point for the national parliaments of sovereign states. The IPU supports contact between parliaments and parliamentarians, and works for the firm establishment of representative democracy by developing under-standing of how representative institutions can be strengthened and encouraged.

liberty (uk)

http://www.liberty-human-rights.org.uk/
Liberty is a membership organisation that seeks to promote and protect human rights and civil liberties in the UK. Liberty under-takes research and advocacy activities, provides advice and training on human rights to lawyers and the public, and tests laws thought to infringe human rights by taking cases to UK and European courts.

national democratic institute for international affairs (us)

http://www.ndi.org
The National Democratic Institute works to strengthen and expand democracy worldwide by providing practical assistance to civic and political leaders advancing democratic values, practices and institu-tions. The NDI is closely linked to the US Democratic Party, but its activities aim to foster universal values and support democratic processes, rather than a particular party or ideology.

national endowment for democracy (us)

http://www.ned.org
The National Endowment for Democracy is a non-profit-making, non-partisan organisation that aims to strengthen democratic insti-tutions around the world. The NED assists new and developing democracies by strengthening the institutions and procedures of electoral democracy to ensure free and fair elections, and encour-aging the gradual consolidation of liberal democracy by measures that strengthen the rule of law, protect individual liberties and foster social pluralism.

ngonet.org

http://www.ngonet.org
NGONet.org is an electronic networking resource for non-governmental organisations in Central and Eastern Europe and the former Soviet Union. Supported by Freedom House (see above) and the US Agency for International Development, NGONet.org encourages cross-border co-operation and communication between Central and East European NGOs, particularly public policy institutes ('think-tanks') and civic activist organisations.

open democracy

http://www.opendemocracy.net
Open Democracy is an Internet-based magazine that aims to encourage the advancement of education and particularly the understanding of democracy, global processes and participation. Open Democracy publishes debates exploring contemporary issues in politics and culture, with the intention of helping people make up their own minds.

open democracy advice centre

http://www.opendemocracy.org.za
The Open Democracy Advice Centre is a South African NGO that aims to encourage open and transparent democracy and foster a culture of corporate and government accountability by promoting rights to freedom of information.

operation black vote

http://www.obv.org.uk
Operation Black Vote is the United Kingdom's only national Black policy research and networking organisation focused on broad-based issues. OBV actively promotes better co-operation between Black and White through political education and encouraging participation and fair representation, with the aim of giving African, Asian and Caribbean communities a louder voice.

public citizen

http://www.citizen.org
Public Citizen is a US American advocacy organisation that demands openness and transparency in government, and

campaigns for justice in sustainable development, trade and welfare issues.

social watch

http://www.socialwatch.org
Social Watch is an international network of citizens' groups which aims to promote the fulfilment of internationally agreed commitments on poverty eradication and equality. Social Watch groups are organised nationally on an ad hoc basis to lobby and hold them accountable, and to promote dialogue about the national social development priorities, particularly by publishing an annual country report. The international secretariat of Social Watch is hosted by the Third World Institute in Montevideo, Uruguay.

statewatch

http://www.statewatch.org
Statewatch monitors the actions of European governments and the European Union, analysing their impact on justice, civil liberties, accountability and openness. Statewatch aims to encourage informed discussion and debate by providing news, features and analyses of governments' actions; it also provides full-text primary sources so that people can easily access documents and draw their own conclusions.

the center for public integrity

http://www.publicintegrity.org
The Center for Public Integrity investigates and reports on public policy issues in the USA and around the world. By publicising issues such as the power of money in politics, the Center aims to help citizens become more informed about their government and subsequently demand greater accountability from officials and elected politicians. The Center has established a network of investigative journalists pursuing similar aims in approximately fifty countries.

transparency international

http://www.transparency.org
Transparency International is a non-governmental organisation devoted to combating corruption. Transparency International works

at national and international levels in eighty-five countries around the world to raise awareness about the damaging effects of corruption, to increase accountability and transparency in public and commercial life, and to advocate reforms and the observance of existing laws.

west african ngo network

http://www.wangonet.org
The West African NGO Network (WANGONeT) is an electronic community of civil society organisation across West Africa. WANGONeT aims to enable communication between regional member NGOs by providing training, infrastructure and expertise to make the Internet accessible.

westminster foundation for democracy (uk)

http://www.wfd.org
The Westminster Foundation for Democracy provides technical assistance to strengthen democratic institutions and values in middle-income and developing countries around the world. Its main areas of interest are political parties, parliaments, legal reform, the media, human rights, electoral administration and Trade Unions. The Westminster Foundation is funded by the UK Government, and the three main UK political parties are each represented on its Board of Governors.

world social forum

http://www.forumsocialmondial.br
The World Social Forum is an organisation of groups and movements from around the world committed to building a global society based around respect for human rights, social justice and democracy and the environment. Groups in the World Social Forum share and develop ideas and practices on how to counter the effects of neo-liberal social and economic development.

worldwatch institute

http://www.worldwatch.org
The WorldWatch Institute is an independent research organisation that works for an environmentally sustainable and socially just

society, in which the needs of all people are met without threatening the health of the natural environment or the well-being of future generations.

datasets on democracy and public opinion

freedom house

http://www.freedomhouse.org/research/survey2004.htm
Annual index of freedom in civil and political rights, covering almost two hundred countries.

global-barometer

http://www.globalbarometer.org
Detailed annual survey data on public attitudes to democracy and political change, covering fifty-six countries in Africa, Asia, Central and Eastern Europe and Latin America.

polity iv dataset, university of maryland

http://www.cidcm.umd.edu/inscr/polity
Dataset of annual information on the characteristics of governments (political regimes) and of their authority covering two hundred countries.

the united nations affinity data project

http://www.vanderbilt.edu/%7Ertucker/data/affinity/un/similar
A dataset capturing the similarity of foreign policy positions based on states' votes and resolutions at the UN General Assembly (between 1946 and 1996).

world bank governance indicators dataset

http://www.worldbank.org/wbi/governance/govdata2002
Dataset of estimates covering six dimensions of governance (participation and accountability; political stability and absence of violence; government effectiveness; regulatory quality; rule of law; control of corruption) for two hundred countries.

index

Note: *italicised* page numbers refer to tables and figures.